AMERICAN GARDENS

1890–1930

NORTHEAST, MID-ATLANTIC, AND MIDWEST REGIONS

AMERICAN GARDENS

1890–1930

EDITED, WITH AN INTRODUCTION BY SAM WATTERS

ACANTHUS PRESS

NEW YORK : 2006

ACANTHUS PRESS, LLC
48 WEST 22ND STREET
NEW YORK, NEW YORK 10010
WWW.ACANTHUSPRESS.COM
212-414-0108

Library of Congress Cataloging-in-Publication Data
American gardens, 1890–1930 : Northeast, Mid-Atlantic, and Midwest /
edited and with an introduction by Sam Watters.
    p. cm.
  Includes bibliographical references (p.   ) and index.
  ISBN 0-926494-43-0 (alk. paper)
  1. Gardens—Northeastern States—Pictorial works. 2. Gardens—
Middle Atlantic States—Pictorial works. 3. Gardens—Middle West—
Pictorial works. I. Watters, Sam, 1954–

SB466.U65N7521 2006
712.0973—dc22
                    2006013759

PHOTOGRAPHY CREDITS
*Photographs are courtesy of and used by permission of the following
(all rights reserved):* pages 134, 177 Lake Forest-Lake Bluff Historical Society;
135, 148 Art Institute of Chicago, Historic Architecture and Landscape Image
Collection, Ryerson and Burnham Archives; 136–137 Chicago Historical Society
(Hedrich Blessing); 140–143 Lake Forest Preservation Foundation; 146–147
Glencoe Historical Society; 178 Architectural Record; 204, 247, 248, 251 The
Trustees of Reservations; and 205 Frederic Law Olmsted National Historic Site.

COVER: *Garden View,* studio of Gertrude Vanderbilt Whitney; Leavitt & Aldrich,
landscape architects; Delano & Aldrich, architects

FRONTISPIECE: *Garden from the Terrace,* "Naumkeag"; Nathan Franklin Barrett,
landscape architect; Stanford White, architect

BACK COVER: *View to the Garden,* Estate of Herbert Croly; Charles Adams Platt,
architect and landscape architect

BARRY CENOWER, PUBLISHER
POLLY FRANCHINI, DESIGNER

PRINTED IN CHINA

Contents

From 1890 to 1930, American landscape architecture flourished as an independent discipline concurrent with its long-established counterpart, building architecture. To recognize the alliance between these two design professions, Acanthus Press is publishing three volumes on American residential garden architecture to parallel its series on Urban and Suburban Domestic Architecture of the Great House era.

Finley Barrell House   Lake Forest, Illinois   Howard Van Doren Shaw, architect   Warren Manning, landscape architect   Sun Porch View to Garden

Introduction

ANDREW JACKSON DOWNING (1815–1852) was the first American-born landscape architect, and his *Treatise on the Theory and Practice of Landscape Gardening, Adapted to North America; with a View to the Improvement of Country Residences* was an influential exploration of American solutions to garden design. Published in 1841, the *Treatise* went into eight editions. By 1890, America's love of gardening and all things natural—lying beyond the controlling and, by implication, corrupting forces of civilization—was in full bloom. Incorporating not only romantic ideas of the good domestic life but beliefs in the social benefits that nature could bring to an increasingly industrialized society, theorists, critics, and designers seized on gardens and the activity of gardening as beneficial to the physical and moral health of the nation. Landscape design became firmly allied with the architectural planning of both private properties and expanded city plans, most notably in the pioneering work of Frederick Law Olmsted (1822–1903). His farsighted orchestration of large spaces that evoked profound visual and psychological experiences defined a uniquely American landscape design that sought to enhance urban living.

Turn-of-the-century cultural and economic forces coalesced to bring the moral benefits of gardening to the lives of many Americans. In the 1870s and 1880s, suburbanization of the immediate outlying countryside of American cities began in earnest. With the overall rise in living standards brought on by post–Civil War prosperity, the dream of owning a house outside congested city centers became a reality. While middle-class neighborhoods were formed through the layout of tree-lined streets and side-by-side lots, larger estate areas for the upper classes emerged, permitting private properties with communal riding trails and clubhouses for like-minded neighbors.

Vast estates preceded smaller developments of 10- to 50-acre parcels close enough to major cities to permit weekend sojourns and summer vacations. With the expansion of national parkways and the increased viability of automobile travel, some of these properties would become permanent residences. In the East and Midwest, wealthy social leaders, politicians, and industrialists formed lavish country estates from undeveloped scenic farmlands. Country divertissements included the breeding of cows, sheep, and dogs, and sports such as golf, tennis, and horseback riding. As the century progressed, the design and care of gardens were added to the list of suitable country house activities for women.

Although architects such as Carrère & Hastings and Wilson Eyre designed the gardens and houses of major projects, the turn-of-the-century building boom created a demand for the independent landscape architect working in tandem with the building architect. Major universities including Harvard and MIT founded schools of landscape architecture. Because these schools did not accept women in the early 20th century, design schools were formed by women themselves. By the 1920s, Beatrix Farrand, the niece of Edith Wharton—herself a contemporary arbiter of taste—Ellen Shipman, and Marian Coffin rivaled male counterparts who, nonetheless, continued to receive the majority of commissions. Housewives and women professionals expanded their voice in horticultural matters with the founding in 1913 of the influential Garden Club of America that eventually affiliated thousands of regional gardening clubs.

Nurseries proliferated both nationally and internationally in the 19th century, and American gardens were planted with native American species augmented by a remarkable array of plants assembled from around the world. With the advancement in greenhouse design and manufacturing, estate owners hired private horticulturalists to collect rare plants in South America and Asia. Exotic orchids dislodged from Amazon tree trunks and Himalayan primroses from Nepalese mountain streams were shipped back by plant collectors to acquisitive estate owners. These exotic treasures were hoarded and cultivated in elaborate glass houses integrated into country estate plans.

Nurseries hired trained plantsmen to assist a growing clientele of landscape architects and house owners. Often trained in European botanical gardens that housed the earliest specimen plant collections, these men were not only essential participants in the estate garden design process, but they also designed gardens for property owners without the intermediary of a landscape architect. After the initial planting of a property, some project supervisors were hired by their clients to manage the gardening staff and oversee the inevitable ongoing redesign of estate parks and planting beds.

Periodicals and books devoted to gardens and country living flourished during the period. *House & Garden, The House Beautiful,* and *Country Life in America* were launched, presenting not only profiles of gardens and gardening tips, but articles defining the well-lived country life. These general interest publications were joined by more professionally oriented publications—*Garden and Forest, Pacific Gardener, The National Horticultural Magazine*—that addressed specific horticultural and design issues.

A national pride of place gave rise to elegant picture books featuring primarily the great estates of the Northeast. Seductive to the outsider, affirming to the property owner, and client-building for the architects, these books profiled, through black and white photographs, estate gardens and their houses. With limited introductory text and absent of owner portraits or biographies, illustrated books evoked the hushed life of the rich American at home in the country. Among the most lavish and successful of these books were *American Gardens* (1902) by the architect and landscape designer Guy Lowell; *American Estates and Gardens* (1904) by architectural critic Barr Ferree; *American Homes of To-day* (1924) by journalist Augusta Owen Patterson; and *American Landscape Architecture* (1924) by P. H. Elwood Jr., landscape architect and the founder of Iowa State University's influential department of landscape architecture. It is from these books and others that Acanthus Press has assembled this presentation of American gardens, re-creating through traditional book design and archival photographs the seductive allure of the original volumes.

As we do today, when Americans opened these earlier books they found an astounding and perhaps enviable world of English castles, French chateaux, and Italian palazzos set into the American

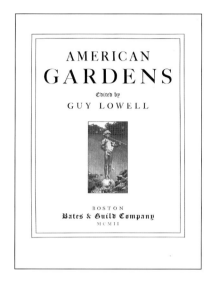 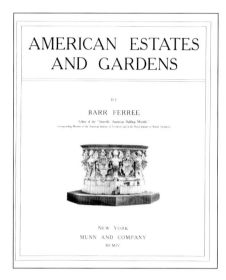 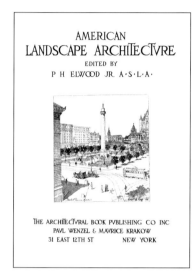 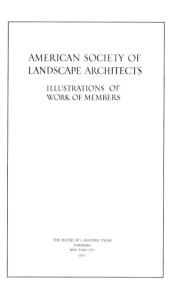

Title pages from: *American Gardens,* by Guy Lowell, 1902; *American Estates and Gardens* by Barr Ferree, 1904; *American Landscape Architecture* by P. H. Elwood Jr., 1924; and the *American Society of Landscape Architects: Illustrations of Work of Members,* 1931.

countryside. Baronial and lavish with elaborate formal gardens, the first grand estates were developed on a grand scale. These houses were intended not just as private retreats but as public displays of wealth and position, dramatically reflecting a new generation's insecurity at a time of great social change and of unprecedented accumulation of private riches. In bold gestures, estate houses and their gardens made aristocrats of their modern-day plutocrat owners. The historicism inherent in their design was the logical outcome not only of the Beaux-Arts training of estate architects but the social aspirations of their rich clients who had been taking the Grand Tour since the 19th century. Just as Rockefeller, Frick, and Kahn came to rule the American economy, so too did their estates exercise dramatic control over the forces of the unbridled American landscape.

The grand European estate was not the only model for the American country house. As the century ended, a movement toward simplicity and informality in both house and landscape design evolved. The casual English country way of life came to the fore, reflected in the architecture and garden design of Georgian brick houses, rusticated half-timber Tudor buildings, and Colonial Revival "farmhouses" with white clapboard siding and dark shutters.

Eclecticism and the blending of traditional sources characterized both residential and landscape design at the turn of the century. Formal Continental traditions, English Arts and Crafts gardens, and the pioneering work of Charles Platt and his circle at Cornish, New Hampshire, were sources for the American landscape designer. The integration of house and garden, of interior and exterior spaces, became a defining idea in American landscape theory. Sites were carefully considered for their particular aspect, and consideration was given to both aesthetic and practical demands. Plans used formal architectonic garden elements—axial walks, multilevel terraces, and geometric planting beds—as transitions to a landscape's more naturalistic effects. Never slavish in their use of traditional elements, landscape architects creatively combined classical pergolas, Italianate pavilions, and formal water elements with rose arbors, herbaceous borders, and dirt pathways. The country house garden was intended for the experience, however manifested, of nature. It was to be walked in, meditated on, and cultivated, not just observed.

The Depression closed the Great House and garden era. Taxes, a declining population of servants, and shifts in taste and ways of living made the large country house a luxury of the past. The legacy of this era is the continued examination and elaboration of the relationship of house to garden. The importance of site and the concept of the garden as an outdoor room to be defined volumetrically through plant selection and architecture continue to influence and define the evolution of American landscape design.

AMERICAN GARDENS

1890–1930

KEY TO THE CAPTIONS

Name of landscape architect or firm appears at the tops of pages.

Caption information (when known) is listed below photographs in the following order :

ESTATE NAME, NAME OF CLIENT, LOCATION, HOUSE ARCHITECT, *Name of Garden View or Plan*

CORNISH, NEW HAMPSHIRE   *Flower Garden*

"SHADOW BROOK"   DR. ERNEST FAHNESTOCK   SHREWSBURY, NEW JERSEY   ALBRO & LINDEBERG   *Rear Terrace*

ESTATE OF DR. F. K. HOLLISTER   EAST HAMPTON, NEW YORK   ALBRO & LINDEBERG   *Garden Facade*

ESTATE OF THOMAS H. KERR   WHITE PLAINS, NEW YORK   ALBRO & LINDEBERG   *The Formal Garden*

ESTATE OF JAMES A. STILLMAN   POCANTICO HILLS, NEW YORK   ALBRO & LINDEBERG   *Garden Facade*

"ROHALLION"   EDWARD DEAN ADAMS   SEA BRIGHT, NEW JERSEY   McKIM, MEAD & WHITE   *Sculpture of Pan; Inset: Plan*

"ROHALLION"   EDWARD DEAN ADAMS   SEA BRIGHT, NEW JERSEY   McKIM, MEAD & WHITE   *Sand Garden*

"NAUMKEAG" JOSEPH H. CHOATE STOCKBRIDGE, MASSACHUSETTS STANFORD WHITE *Garden Facade*

"NAUMKEAG"   JOSEPH H. CHOATE   STOCKBRIDGE, MASSACHUSETTS   STANFORD WHITE   *Along the Terrace*

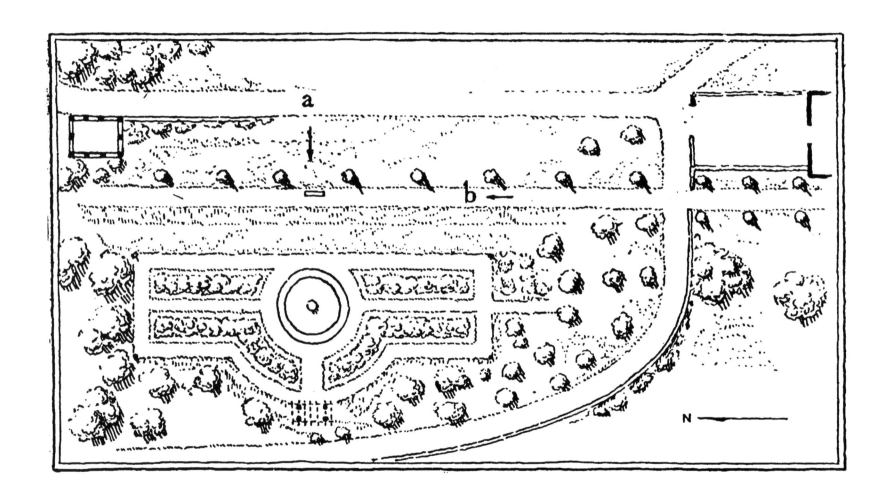

"NAUMKEAG"   JOSEPH H. CHOATE   STOCKBRIDGE, MASSACHUSETTS   STANFORD WHITE   *Plan*

ESTATE OF GEORGE BRAMWELL BAKER   CHESTNUT HILL, MASSACHUSETTS   *Grass Walk*

"HARBOUR COURT"   MRS. JOHN NICHOLAS BROWN   NEWPORT, RHODE ISLAND   RALPH ADAMS CRAM   *Entrance to Lower Garden*

ESTATE OF WILLIAM ELLERY   BROOKLINE, MASSACHUSETTS   *Garden House*

"KYKUIT"   JOHN D. ROCKEFELLER   POCANTICO HILLS, NEW YORK   WELLES BOSWORTH   *Main Entrance*

"KYKUIT"   JOHN D. ROCKEFELLER   POCANTICO HILLS, NEW YORK   WELLES BOSWORTH   *Aerial View of House and Gardens*

"KYKUIT"   JOHN D. ROCKEFELLER   POCANTICO HILLS, NEW YORK   WELLES BOSWORTH   *Left: Fountain of Oceanus; Right: Allée*

"KYKUIT"   JOHN D. ROCKEFELLER   POCANTICO HILLS, NEW YORK   WELLES BOSWORTH   *The Brook Garden*

"KYKUIT"   JOHN D. ROCKEFELLER   POCANTICO HILLS, NEW YORK   WELLES BOSWORTH   *Japanese Garden*

"KYKUIT"   JOHN D. ROCKEFELLER   POCANTICO HILLS, NEW YORK   WELLES BOSWORTH   *Pool*

"KYKUIT"   JOHN D. ROCKEFELLER   POCANTICO HILLS, NEW YORK   WELLES BOSWORTH   *Terrace Stairway*

"KYKUIT"   JOHN D. ROCKEFELLER   POCANTICO HILLS, NEW YORK   WELLES BOSWORTH   *Fountain*

"GREYSTONE"   SAMUEL UNTERMYER   YONKERS, NEW YORK   WELLES BOSWORTH   *Open Temple*

"GREYSTONE"   SAMUEL UNTERMYER   YONKERS, NEW YORK   WELLES BOSWORTH   *Left: Walk to Hudson River; Right: Lawn Terrace*

"THE ELMS"   EDWARD J. BERWIND   NEWPORT, RHODE ISLAND   HORACE TRUMBAUER   *Garden Facade*

"THE ELMS"   EDWARD J. BERWIND   NEWPORT, RHODE ISLAND   HORACE TRUMBAUER   *Garden Terrace*

ESTATE OF KENT FULTON   SACHEMS HEAD, CONNECTICUT   GALZIER & BROOKS   *Entrance and Terrace*

"GLYNALLEN"   GEORGE MARSHALL ALLEN   CONVENT, NEW JERSEY   CHARLES I. BERG   *Canal and Walled Pergola*

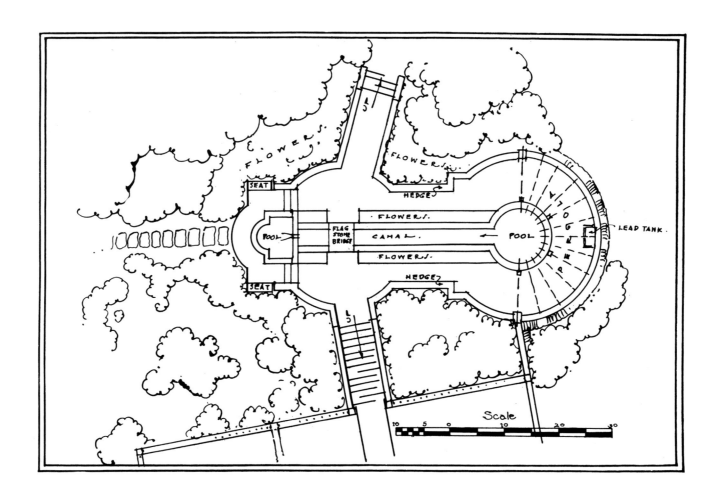

"GLYNALLEN"   GEORGE MARSHALL ALLEN   CONVENT, NEW JERSEY   CHARLES I. BERG   *Sketch of the Garden*

"DOLOBRAN"   FRANCES C. GRISCOM   HAVERFORD, PENNSYLVANIA   FURNESS–EVANS   *Pool and Garden Wall*

ESTATE OF HUGH BANCROFT   COHASSET, MASSACHUSETTS   *Garden and Swimming Pool*

"INDIAN HARBOR"   ELIAS C. BENEDICT   GREENWICH, CONNECTICUT   CARRÈRE & HASTINGS   *West Shore Looking North*

"INDIAN HARBOR"   ELIAS C. BENEDICT   GREENWICH, CONNECTICUT   CARRÈRE & HASTINGS   *The Flower Garden*

"INDIAN HARBOR"   ELIAS C. BENEDICT   GREENWICH, CONNECTICUT   CARRÈRE & HASTINGS   *Left: Boat Landing; Right: Pergola*

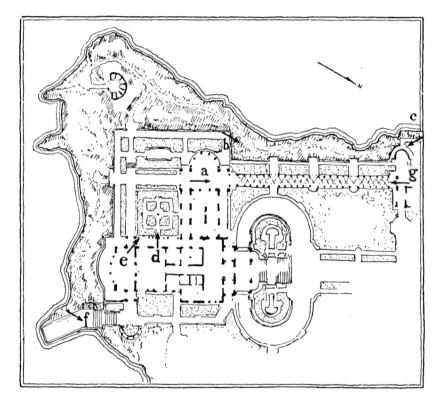

"INDIAN HARBOR"   ELIAS C. BENEDICT   GREENWICH, CONNECTICUT   CARRÈRE & HASTINGS   *Left: Pergola from the Portico; Right: Plan*

"ELLIS COURT"   FREDERICK CROMWELL   BERNARDSVILLE, NEW JERSEY   CARRÈRE & HASTINGS   *The Lower Garden*

"ELLIS COURT"   FREDERICK CROMWELL   BERNARDSVILLE, NEW JERSEY   CARRÈRE & HASTINGS   *Left: View From Veranda; Right: Veranda*

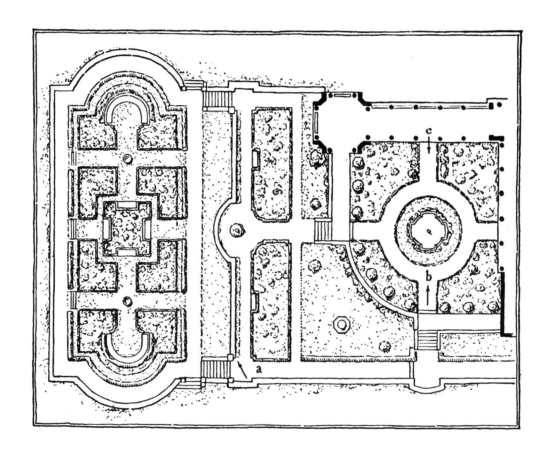

"ELLIS COURT"   FREDERICK CROMWELL   BERNARDSVILLE, NEW JERSEY   CARRÈRE & HASTINGS   *Plan*

"NEMOURS"   ALFRED I. DuPONT   WILMINGTON, DELAWARE   CARRÈRE & HASTINGS   *Terrace*

"KNOLE"   HERMAN B. DURYEA   WESTBURY, LONG ISLAND   CARRÈRE & HASTINGS   *Allée*

"BELLEFONTAINE" GIRAUD FOSTER   LENOX, MASSACHUSETTS   CARRÈRE & HASTINGS   *Garden Facade*

"BELLEFONTAINE"   GIRAUD FOSTER   LENOX, MASSACHUSETTS   CARRÈRE & HASTINGS   *Water Garden Looking to House*

"BELLEFONTAINE"   GIRAUD FOSTER   LENOX, MASSACHUSETTS   CARRÈRE & HASTINGS   *Water Garden from House*

"BELLEFONTAINE"   GIRAUD FOSTER   LENOX, MASSACHUSETTS   CARRÈRE & HASTINGS   *Left: Faun Fountain; Right: East Flower Garden*

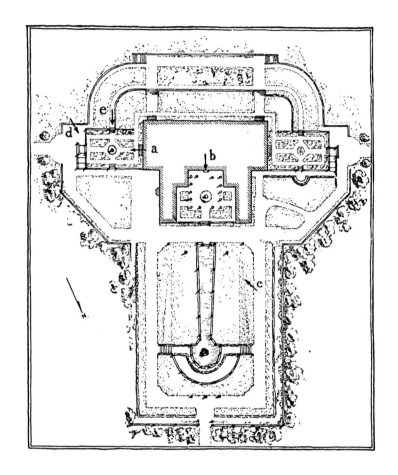

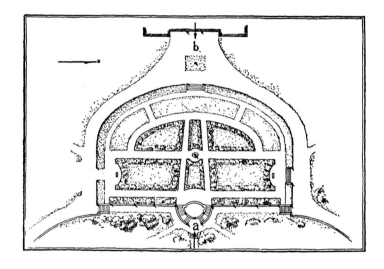

CARRÈRE & HASTINGS   *Left: "BELLEFONTAINE" Plan; Right: "BURRWOOD" Plan*

"BURRWOOD"   WALTER JENNINGS   COLD SPRING HARBOR, NEW YORK   CARRÈRE & HASTINGS   *Garden Facade*

"BURRWOOD"   WALTER JENNINGS   COLD SPRING HARBOR, NEW YORK   CARRÈRE & HASTINGS   *Sunken Garden*

"CEDAR COURT"   OTTO KAHN   MORRISTOWN, NEW JERSEY   CARRÈRE & HASTINGS   *Courtyard*

"CEDAR COURT"   OTTO KAHN   MORRISTOWN, NEW JERSEY   CARRÈRE & HASTINGS   *Left: Sunken Pool; Right: Pergola Opposite Entrance*

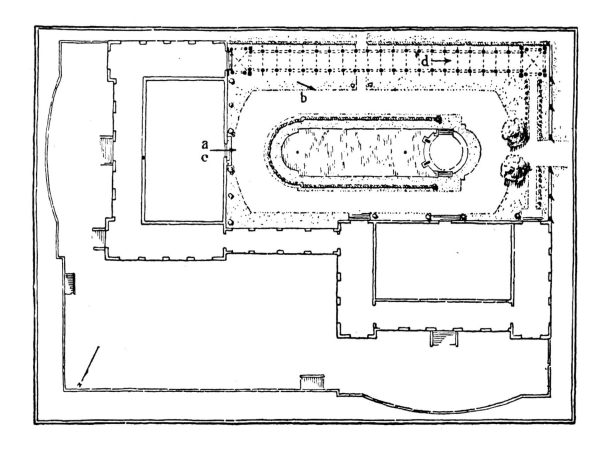

"CEDAR COURT" OTTO KAHN MORRISTOWN, NEW JERSEY CARRÈRE & HASTINGS *Plan*

"INDIAN HARBOR"   DONALDSON BROWN   ARDSLEY, NEW YORK   *Steps to Water Terrace*

"HOPEDENE"   E. H. G. SLATER   NEWPORT, RHODE ISLAND   PEABODY & STEARNS   *Entrance Court*

"HOPEDENE"   E. H. G. SLATER   NEWPORT, RHODE ISLAND   PEABODY & STEARNS   *Garden Facade*

ESTATE OF EDGAR BASSICK   BRIDGEPORT, CONNECTICUT   *Rose Garden*

"FROST MILL LODGE"   IRVING BROKAW   MILL NECK, NEW YORK   HORACE TRUMBAUER   *View of Pool from Terrace*

"BRYCE HOUSE" LLOYD BRYCE ROSLYN, NEW YORK OGDEN CODMAN *Garden Facade*

"BRYCE HOUSE"   LLOYD BRYCE   ROSLYN, NEW YORK   OGDEN CODMAN   *Terrace*

"WHITE WINGS"   FREDERICK FREYLINGHUYSEN   ELBERON, NEW JERSEY   *Boxwood Garden*

"BAYBERRY LAND"   CHARLES H. SABIN   SOUTHAMPTON, NEW YORK   CROSS & CROSS   *Aerial View*

"BAYBERRY LAND"   CHARLES H. SABIN   SOUTHAMPTON, NEW YORK   CROSS & CROSS   *Garden Path*

"BAYBERRY LAND"   CHARLES H. SABIN   SOUTHAMPTON, NEW YORK   CROSS & CROSS   *Entrance Court*

"GIBRALTAR"   H. RODNEY SHARP   WILMINGTON, DELAWARE   *Main Garden*

"GIBRALTAR"   H. RODNEY SHARP   WILMINGTON, DELAWARE   *Evergreen Terrace*

ESTATE OF GEORGE MABEE   NEW HAVEN, CONNECTICUT   DOUGLASS ORR   *Flower Garden*

ESTATE OF WARREN C. KINNEY   MORRISTOWN, NEW JERSEY   *General View*

"OAK KNOLL"   BERTRAM G. WORK   MILL NECK, NEW YORK   DELANO & ALDRICH   *Fountain Court*

"OAK KNOLL"   BERTRAM G. WORK   MILL NECK, NEW YORK   DELANO & ALDRICH   *Plan*

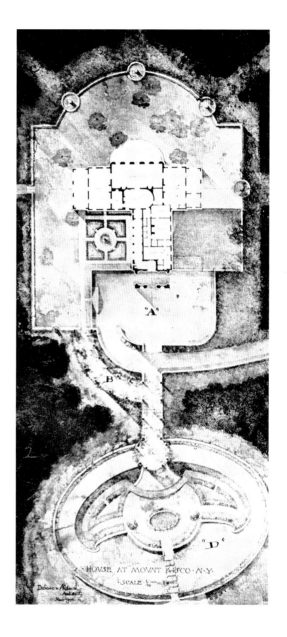

"AVALON" ROBERT S. BREWSTER MT. KISCO, NEW YORK DELANO & ALDRICH *Left: Stair to Temple; Right: Plan*

"AVALON"   ROBERT S. BREWSTER   MT. KISCO, NEW YORK   DELANO & ALDRICH   *Swimming Pool Pavilion*

"AVALON"   ROBERT S. BREWSTER   MT. KISCO, NEW YORK   DELANO & ALDRICH   *Swimming Pool Looking to Garden*

ESTATE OF S. C. ALLYN   DAYTON, OHIO   DWIGHT JAMES BAUM   *Annual and Rose Garden*

ESTATE OF I. UPHAM   THREE RIVERS, MASSACHUSETTS   *Cottage Garden*

ESTATE OF CHARLES L. BORIE   RYDAL, PENNSYLVANIA   WILSON EYRE   *Garden Facade*

ESTATE OF CHARLES L. BORIE   RYDAL, PENNSYLVANIA   WILSON EYRE   *Pool*

ESTATE OF CHARLES L. BORIE   RYDAL, PENNSYLVANIA   WILSON EYRE   *General View*

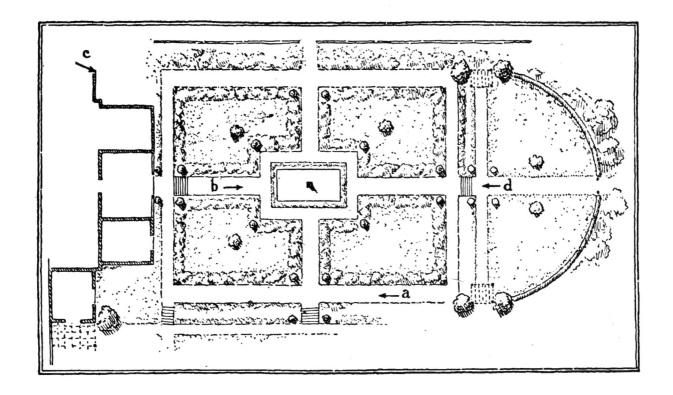

ESTATE OF CHARLES L. BORIE   RYDAL, PENNSYLVANIA   WILSON EYRE   *Plan*

"FAIRACRES"   JOHN W. PEPPER   JENKINTOWN, PENNSYLVANIA   WILSON EYRE   *View of House from Garden*

"FAIRACRES"   JOHN W. PEPPER   JENKINTOWN, PENNSYLVANIA   WILSON EYRE   *General View*

"FAIRACRES"   JOHN W. PEPPER   JENKINTOWN, PENNSYLVANIA   WILSON EYRE   *Garden Lower End*

"FAIRACRES"   JOHN W. PEPPER   JENKINTOWN, PENNSYLVANIA   WILSON EYRE   *Garden Paths*

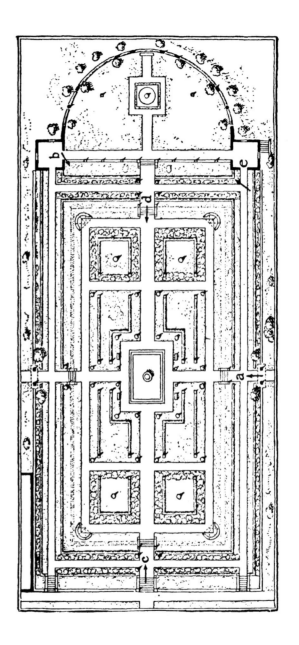

"FAIRACRES"   JOHN W. PEPPER   JENKINTOWN, PENNSYLVANIA   WILSON EYRE   *Left: View of Lilypond; Right: Plan*

"FAIRACRES"   JOHN W. PEPPER   JENKINTOWN, PENNSYLVANIA   WILSON EYRE   *Rendering of House with Gardens*

"ASHFORD"   FRANK SQUIER   BELLE HAVEN, CONNECTICUT   WILSON EYRE   *Left: House Court; Right: Descent to the Garden*

"ASHFORD"   FRANK SQUIER   BELLE HAVEN, CONNECTICUT   WILSON EYRE   *View of the Cutting Garden; Inset: Plan*

"OHEKA" OTTO KAHN COLD SPRING HARBOR, NEW YORK DELANO & ALDRICH *Aerial View*

"OHEKA"   OTTO KAHN   COLD SPRING HARBOR, NEW YORK   DELANO & ALDRICH   *Garden Detail*

"ELMHURST"   WILLARD D. STRAIGHT   OLD WESTBURY, NEW YORK   DELANO & ALDRICH   *Left: Garden Gate; Right: Garden Wall*

"OHEKA"   OTTO KAHN   COLD SPRING HARBOR, NEW YORK   DELANO & ALDRICH   *Garden Detail*

"ELMHURST"   WILLARD D. STRAIGHT   OLD WESTBURY, NEW YORK   DELANO & ALDRICH   *Left: Garden Gate; Right: Garden Wall*

"LILYPOND"   WILLIAM SIMONDS   SOUTHAMPTON, NEW YORK   BRUCE PRICE   *View from Terrace to Pool*

"LILYPOND"   WILLIAM SIMONDS   SOUTHAMPTON, NEW YORK   BRUCE PRICE   *View from Garden*

ESTATE OF B. E. TAYLOR   GROSSE POINTE, MICHIGAN   CHITTENDEN & KOTTING   *Swimming Pool and Tea House*

ESTATE OF B. E. TAYLOR   GROSSE POINTE, MICHIGAN   CHITTENDEN & KOTTING   *Tea House Entrance*

"MEUDON"   W. D. GUTHRIE   LOCUST VALLEY, NEW YORK   C. P. H. GILBERT   *Aerial View*

ESTATE OF L. WILPUTTE   NEW ROCHELLE, NEW YORK   *Walled Garden*

ESTATE OF GEORGE M. MOFFETT   ROSLYN, NEW YORK   MOTT SCHMIDT   *Two Views of the Garden with Outbuildings*

ESTATE OF EDWIN TATHAM   KATONAH, NEW YORK   *Formal Lawn*

"GREEN HILL"   ISABELLA STEWART GARDNER   BROOKLINE, MASSACHUSETTS   J.R. COOLIDGE JR.   *Rendering of House*

"GREEN HILL"   ISABELLA STEWART GARDNER   BROOKLINE, MASSACHUSETTS   J.R. COOLIDGE JR.   *Garden Seat*

"GREEN HILL"   ISABELLA STEWART GARDNER   BROOKLINE, MASSACHUSETTS   J.R. COOLIDGE JR.   *Japanese Garden*

"GREEN HILL"   ISABELLA STEWART GARDNER   BROOKLINE, MASSACHUSETTS   J.R. COOLIDGE JR.   *Arbor*

ESTATE OF THOMAS JEFFRESS   RICHMOND, VIRGINIA   *Swimming Pool*

ESTATE OF THOMAS JEFFRESS   RICHMOND, VIRGINIA   *The Four Seasons Garden*

"WHITEMARSH HALL"   EDWARD T. STOTESBURY   WYNDMOOR, PENNSYLVANIA   HORACE TRUMBAUER   *Upper Terrace and Garden Facade*

"WHITEMARSH HALL"   EDWARD T. STOTESBURY   WYNDMOOR, PENNSYLVANIA   HORACE TRUMBAUER   *Garden Facade with Parterre*

"BLAIRSDEN"   C. LEDYARD BLAIR   PEAPACK, NEW JERSEY   CARRÈRE & HASTINGS   *Garden Steps*

"GRAHAMPTON"   H. W. CROFT   GREENWICH, CONNECTICUT   BENNO JANSSEN   *The Long Terrace*

"GRAHAMPTON"   H. W. CROFT   GREENWICH, CONNECTICUT   BENNO JANSSEN   *Left: Terrace Detail; Right: Gateway*

"GRAHAMPTON"   H. W. CROFT   GREENWICH, CONNECTICUT   BENNO JANSSEN   *Shelter*

"THE BRAES"   HERBERT L. PRATT   GLEN COVE, NEW YORK   JAMES BRITE   *Aerial View*

"THE BRAES"   HERBERT L. PRATT   GLEN COVE, NEW YORK   JAMES BRITE   *Left: Entrance Drive; Right: Sunken Garden*

"THE BRAES"   HERBERT L. PRATT   GLEN COVE, NEW YORK   JAMES BRITE   *Garden View*

JACOB SCHIFF   SEA BRIGHT, NEW JERSEY   *Fountain in the Rose Garden*

ESTATE OF EMORY W. CLARK   CANANDAIGUA, NEW YORK   *Left: Japanese Garden; Right: Tea House*

J. H. REVELY HOUSE   KANSAS CITY, MISSOURI   EDWARD TANNER   *Left: Rill from the Evergreen Garden; Right: Sunken Garden*

ESTATE OF O. L. VANLANINGHAM   KANSAS CITY, MISSOURI   *Water Garden*

"BAGATELLE"   THOMAS HASTINGS   OLD WESTBURY, NEW YORK   CARRÈRE & HASTINGS   *Courtyard Detail*

"GLENALLEN"   MRS. FRANCIS F. PRENTISS   CLEVELAND HEIGHTS, OHIO   *Flower Garden*

ESTATE OF J. L. SEVERANCE   CLEVELAND HEIGHTS, OHIO   *Left: Fountain; Right: Sylvan Path Bridge*

"MILL ROAD FARM" ALBERT D. LASKER LAKE FOREST, ILLINOIS DAVID ADLER *Aerial View*

"MILL ROAD FARM"   ALBERT D. LASKER   LAKE FOREST, ILLINOIS   DAVID ADLER   *Garden Facade*

"MILL ROAD FARM"   ALBERT D. LASKER   LAKE FOREST, ILLINOIS   DAVID ADLER   *Pool*

ESTATE OF H. H. HUNNEWELL   WELLESLEY, MASSACHUSETTS   *Italian Garden*

ESTATE OF H. H. HUNNEWELL   WELLESLEY, MASSACHUSETTS   *Pavilion Overlooking Italian Garden and Lake*

ESTATE OF NOBLE B. JUDAH   LAKE FOREST, ILLINOIS   PHILIP LIPPINCOTT GOODWIN   *Aerial View*

ESTATE OF NOBLE B. JUDAH   LAKE FOREST, ILLINOIS   PHILIP LIPPINCOTT GOODWIN   *Garden Facade*

ESTATE OF NOBLE B. JUDAH   LAKE FOREST, ILLINOIS   PHILIP LIPPINCOTT GOODWIN   *Garden*

ESTATE OF NOBLE B. JUDAH   LAKE FOREST, ILLINOIS   PHILIP LIPPINCOTT GOODWIN   *Orangerie*

"ALL VIEW"   C. OLIVER ISELIN   NEW ROCHELLE, NEW YORK   SIDNEY STRATTON   *Entrance Courtyard*

"ALL VIEW"   C. OLIVER ISELIN   NEW ROCHELLE, NEW YORK   SIDNEY STRATTON   *Formal Garden*

"INDIANOLA"   HERMANN PAEPCKE   GLENCOE, ILLINOIS   FROMMANN & JEBSEN   *Pond*

"HAVENWOOD"   EDWARD RYERSON   LAKE FOREST, ILLINOIS   HOWARD VAN DOREN SHAW   *Pool and Fountain*

"HAVENWOOD"   EDWARD RYERSON   LAKE FOREST, ILLINOIS   HOWARD VAN DOREN SHAW   *Rear Terrace*

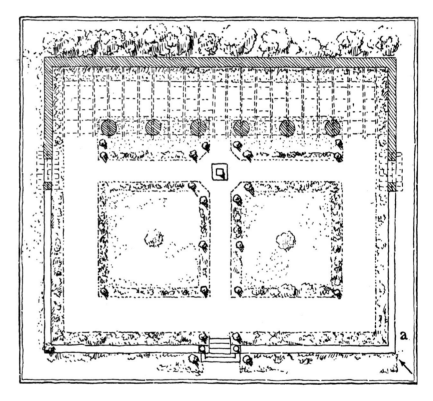

"BRANDYWINE FARM"   CHARLES E. MATHER   LENAPE, PENNSYLVANIA   KEEN & MEAD   *Left: Side View of House; Right: Plan*

"BRANDYWINE FARM"   CHARLES E. MATHER   LENAPE, PENNSYLVANIA   KEEN & MEAD   *Gardens Viewed from the House*

"DRUMTHWACKET"   MOSES T. PYNE   PRINCETON, NEW JERSEY   BRADFORD GILBERT   *Garden View*

"DRUMTHWACKET"   MOSES T. PYNE   PRINCETON, NEW JERSEY   BRADFORD GILBERT   *Far End of the Garden*

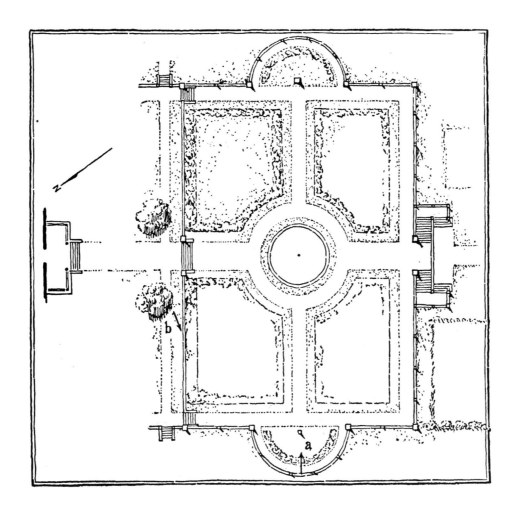

"DRUMTHWACKET"   MOSES T. PYNE   PRINCETON, NEW JERSEY   BRADFORD GILBERT   *Plan*

UNKNOWN ESTATE   BERNARDSVILLE, NEW JERSEY   *Hillside Garden*

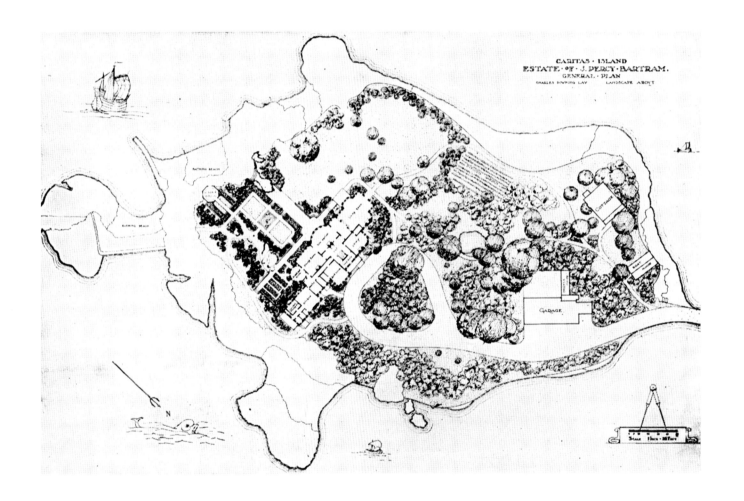

"CARITAS ISLAND" J. PERCY BARTRAM   STAMFORD, CONNECTICUT *Plan*

ESTATE OF CHARLES W. POWER   PITTSFIELD, MASSACHUSETTS   *View of the Shelter*

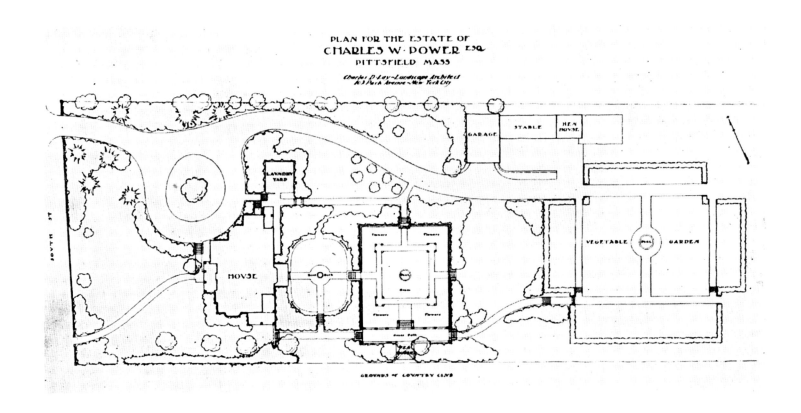

ESTATE OF CHARLES W. POWER   PITTSFIELD, MASSACHUSETTS   *Plan*

"ALLWAYS"   R. H. SIMPSON   OYSTER BAY, NEW YORK   *Garden Detail*

ESTATE OF A. S. STORER   RIDGEFIELD, CONNECTICUT   *Walled Garden*

"THE HEDGES"   WILLIAM C. GALLOWHUR   SCARSDALE, NEW YORK   *Topiary Garden*

"OAK HILL FARM"   J. AMORY HASKELL   RED BANK, NEW JERSEY   *Swimming Pool*

"OAK HILL FARM"   J. AMORY HASKELL   RED BANK, NEW JERSEY   *Left: Iris Garden; Right: Wild Garden*

"OAK HILL FARM"   J. AMORY HASKELL   RED BANK, NEW JERSEY   *Path through the Wild Garden*

STUDIO OF GERTRUDE VANDERBILT WHITNEY   ROSLYN, NEW YORK   DELANO & ALDRICH   *Aerial View*

STUDIO OF GERTRUDE VANDERBILT WHITNEY   ROSLYN, NEW YORK   DELANO & ALDRICH   *Garden View*

STUDIO OF GERTRUDE VANDERBILT WHITNEY   ROSLYN, NEW YORK   DELANO & ALDRICH   *Garden View from the Studio*

"IMMERGRUN"   CHARLES M. SCHWAB   LORETTO, PENNSYLVANIA   *View up Cascade to House*

"IMMERGRUN"   CHARLES M. SCHWAB   LORETTO, PENNSYLVANIA   *View of Pool and Cascade from the House*

"IMMERGRUN"   CHARLES M. SCHWAB   LORETTO, PENNSYLVANIA   *Reflecting Pool with Statuary*

"IMMERGRUN"   CHARLES M. SCHWAB   LORETTO, PENNSYLVANIA   *Blue Jay Gateway*

"IMMERGRUN" CHARLES M. SCHWAB LORETTO, PENNSYLVANIA *Plan*

ESTATE OF ARTHUR S. BURDEN   JERICHO, NEW YORK   JOHN RUSSELL POPE   *Garden with Entrance Gates*

"PENGUIN HALL"   RUBY BOYER MILLER   WENHAM, MASSACHUSETTS   H. T. LINDEBERG   *Garden Facade*

"PENGUIN HALL"   RUBY BOYER MILLER   WENHAM, MASSACHUSETTS   H. T. LINDEBERG   *Garden Detail*

GARDEN IN BEVERLY, MASSACHUSETTS   LITTLE & BROWNE   *Lower Terrace*

GARDEN IN BEVERLY, MASSACHUSETTS   LITTLE & BROWNE   *Fountain Basin*

ESTATE OF FINLEY BARRELL   LAKE FOREST, ILLINOIS   HOWARD VAN DOREN SHAW   *Formal Garden*

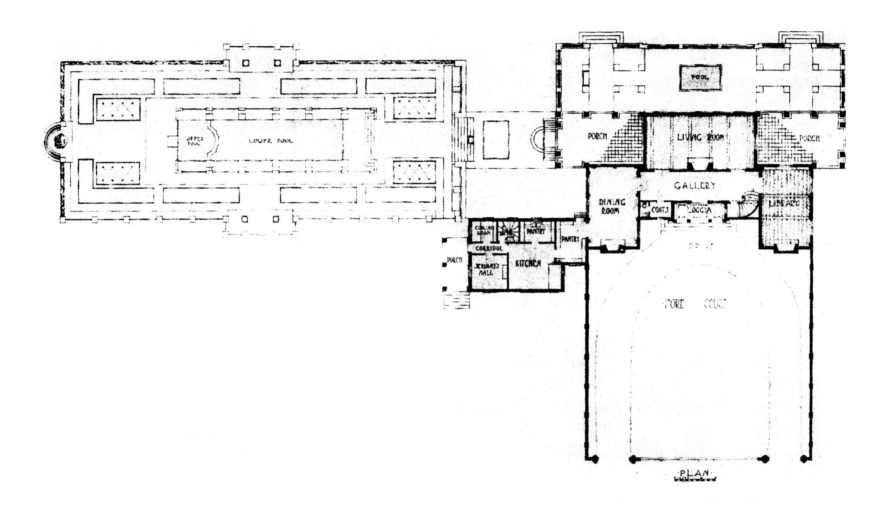

ESTATE OF FINLEY BARRELL   LAKE FOREST, ILLINOIS   HOWARD VAN DOREN SHAW   *Plan*

"WILDWOOD"   CLYDE CARR   LAKE FOREST, ILLINOIS   H. T. LINDEBERG   *View from the Rear Lawn*

ESTATE OF R.T. McCRACKEN   CHESTNUT HILL, PENNSYLVANIA   MELLOR, MEIGS & HOWE   *Escalpier Apple Tree*

ESTATE OF FRANCIS S. McILHENNY   CHESTNUT HILL, PENNSYLVANIA   MELLOR, MEIGS & HOWE   *Left: Forecourt; Right: Lion Fountain*

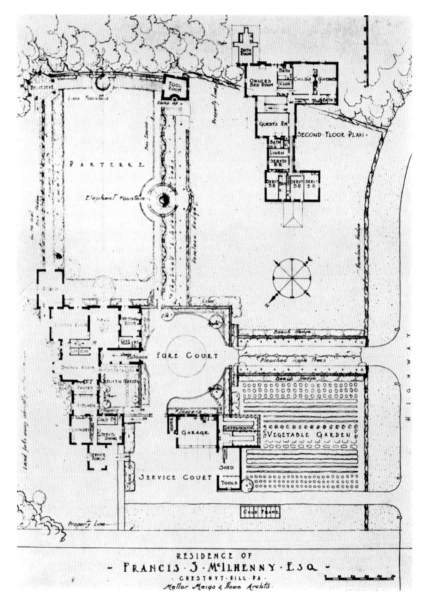

ESTATE OF FRANCIS S. McILHENNY   CHESTNUT HILL, PENNSYLVANIA   MELLOR, MEIGS & HOWE   *Left: Terrace; Right: Plan*

"THE PEAK"   MRS. ARTHUR V. MEIGS   RADNOR, PENNSYLVANIA   MELLOR, MEIGS & HOWE   *Left: Wall Fountain; Right: Dipping Tank*

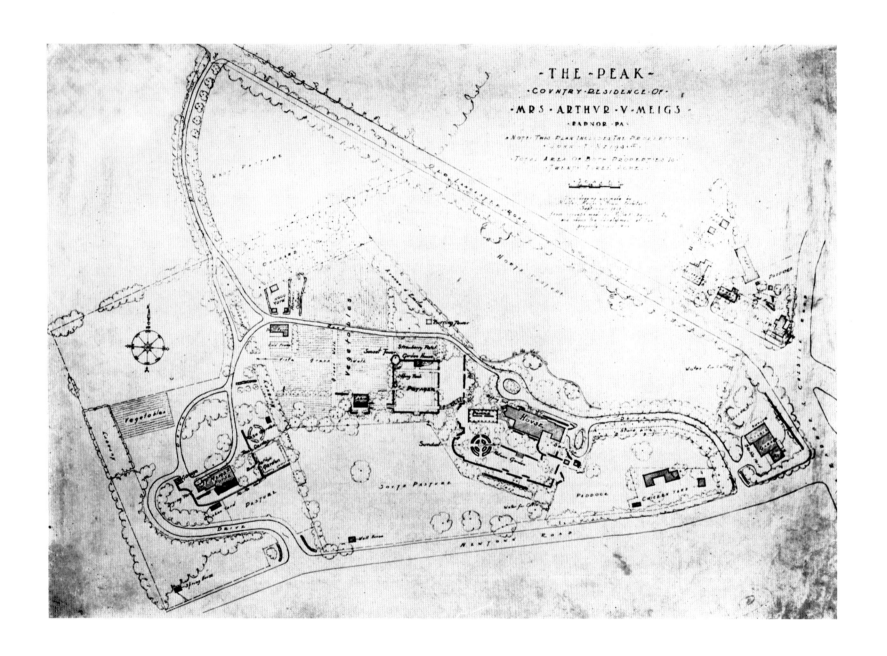

"THE PEAK"   MRS. ARTHUR V. MEIGS   RADNOR, PENNSYLVANIA   MELLOR, MEIGS & HOWE   *Plan*

"NORTHOME"   RUSSELL M. BENNETT   LAKE MINNETONKA, MINNESOTA   *Perennial Garden*

"NORTHOME"   RUSSELL M. BENNETT   LAKE MINNETONKA, MINNESOTA   *Formal Garden*

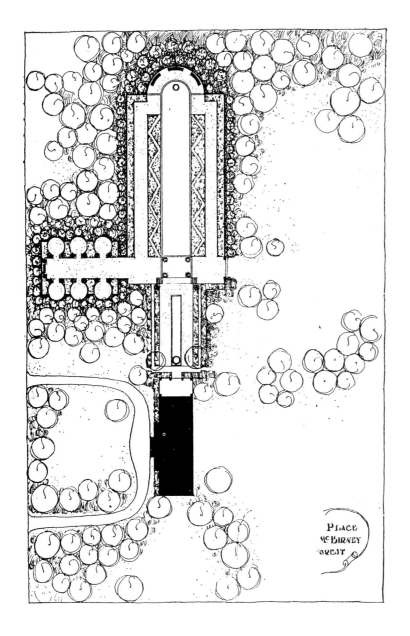

"HOUSE OF THE FOUR WINDS"   HUGH J. McBIRNEY   LAKE FOREST, ILLINOIS   HOWARD VAN DOREN SHAW   *Left: Plan; Right: Water Garden*

"AULDWOOD"   JOSEPH C. HOAGLAND   SEA BRIGHT, NEW JERSEY   SHEPLEY, RUTAN & COOLIDGE   *House Facade*

"AULDWOOD" JOSEPH C. HOAGLAND SEA BRIGHT, NEW JERSEY SHEPLEY, RUTAN & COOLIDGE *Garden Path*

"AULDWOOD"   JOSEPH C. HOAGLAND   SEA BRIGHT, NEW JERSEY   SHEPLEY, RUTAN & COOLIDGE   *Left: Garden; Right: Garden Gate*

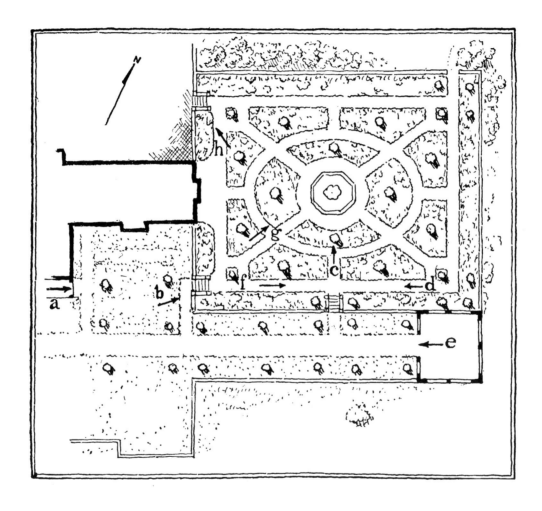

"AULDWOOD"   JOSEPH C. HOAGLAND   SEA BRIGHT, NEW JERSEY   SHEPLEY, RUTAN & COOLIDGE   *Plan*

"AULDWOOD"   JOSEPH C. HOAGLAND   SEA BRIGHT, NEW JERSEY   SHEPLEY, RUTAN & COOLIDGE   *General View*

"OPHIR FARM" WHITELAW REID PURCHASE, NEW YORK McKIM, MEAD & WHITE *Entrance Facade*

"OPHIR FARM"   WHITELAW REID   PURCHASE, NEW YORK   McKIM, MEAD & WHITE   *General View; Inset: Plan*

"BILTMORE"   GEORGE W. VANDERBILT   ASHEVILLE, NORTH CAROLINA   RICHARD MORRIS HUNT   *Pools and Garden*

"WOODLEA"   ELLIOTT SHEPARD   SCARBOROUGH, NEW YORK   McKIM, MEAD & WHITE   *House from Garden Fountain*

"WOODLEA"   ELLIOTT SHEPARD   SCARBOROUGH, NEW YORK   McKIM, MEAD & WHITE   *Fountain Detail*

"WOODLEA"   ELLIOTT SHEPARD   SCARBOROUGH, NEW YORK   McKIM, MEAD & WHITE   *Left: Terrace Steps; Right: Fountain and Pergola*

"WOODLEA" ELLIOTT SHEPARD SCARBOROUGH, NEW YORK McKIM, MEAD & WHITE *Left: Italian Wellhead; Right: Bed of Evergreens*

"WOODLEA"   ELLIOTT SHEPARD   SCARBOROUGH, NEW YORK   McKIM, MEAD & WHITE   *Garden from the Terrace*

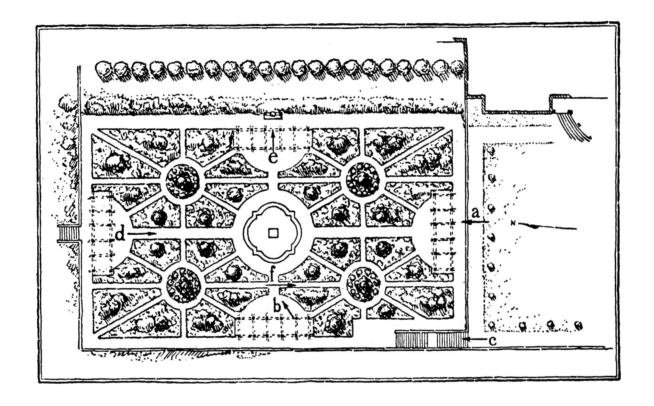

"WOODLEA"   ELLIOTT SHEPARD   SCARBOROUGH, NEW YORK   McKIM, MEAD & WHITE   *Plan*

"ORMSTON"   JOHN E. ALDRED   LATTINGTOWN, NEW YORK   BERTRAM G. GOODHUE   *Aerial View*

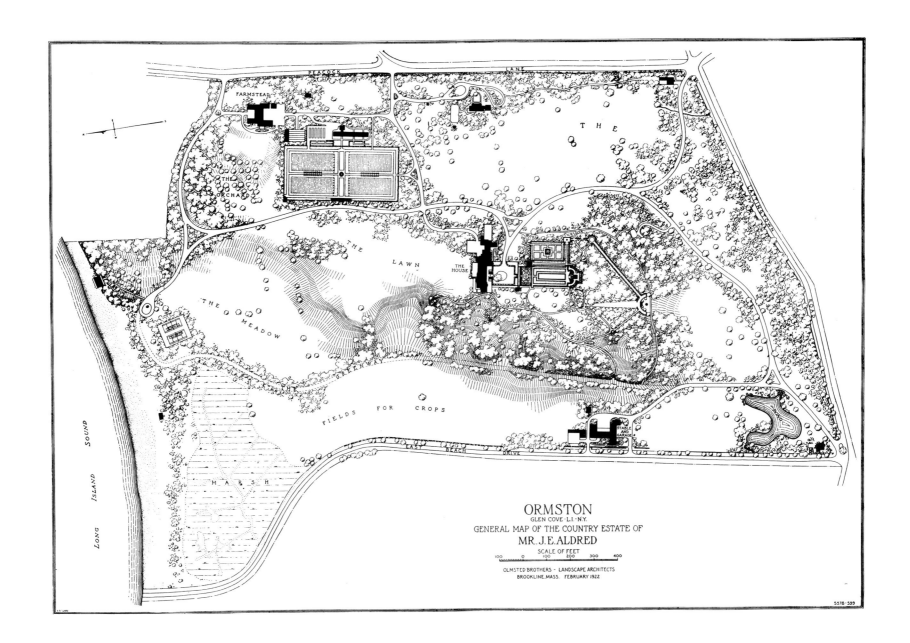

"ORMSTON"   JOHN E. ALDRED   LATTINGTOWN, NEW YORK   BERTRAM G. GOODHUE   *Plan*

"CASTLE HILL"   R. T. CRANE   IPSWICH, MASSACHUSETTS   PEABODY & STEARNS   *Left: Italian Garden Fountain; Right: Fountain detail*

"CASTLE HILL"   R. T. CRANE   IPSWICH, MASSACHUSETTS   PEABODY & STEARNS   *Italian Garden*

"RONAELE MANOR"   FITZ EUGENE DIXON   ELKINS PARK, PENNSYLVANIA   HORACE TRUMBAUER   *Garden Facade*

"BEACON HILL HOUSE" ARTHUR CURTISS JAMES NEWPORT, RHODE ISLAND HOWELLS & STOKES *Outbuildings and Vegetable Gardens*

"BEACON HILL HOUSE" ARTHUR CURTISS JAMES NEWPORT, RHODE ISLAND HOWELLS & STOKES *Approach to the Garden*

"BEACON HILL HOUSE"   ARTHUR CURTISS JAMES   NEWPORT, RHODE ISLAND   HOWELLS & STOKES   *Long Pool in the Blue Garden*

"BLACK POINT"   H. H. ROGERS   SOUTHAMPTON, NEW YORK   WALKER & GILLETTE   *Left: Garden Entrance; Right: Garden Theater*

"BLACK POINT"   H. H. ROGERS   SOUTHAMPTON, NEW YORK   WALKER & GILLETTE   *Garden Wall*

ESTATE OF HENRY R. REA   SEWICKLEY, PENNSYLVANIA   HISS & WEEKES   *View of the Topiary Garden*

"THE WELD"   LARS ANDERSON   BROOKLINE, MASSACHUSETTS   *Gazebo Detail*

"THE WELD"   LARS ANDERSON   BROOKLINE, MASSACHUSETTS   *Fountain*

ESTATE OF HERBERT CROLY   CORNISH, NEW HAMPSHIRE   CHARLES ADAMS PLATT   *View to House*

ESTATE OF HERBERT CROLY   CORNISH, NEW HAMPSHIRE   CHARLES ADAMS PLATT   *View to Garden*

"VILLA TURICUM" HAROLD McCORMICK   LAKE FOREST, ILLINOIS   CHARLES ADAMS PLATT   *Water Stairs*

ESTATE OF CHARLES ADAMS PLATT   CORNISH, NEW HAMPSHIRE   CHARLES ADAMS PLATT   *Front Stair*

ESTATE OF CHARLES ADAMS PLATT   CORNISH, NEW HAMPSHIRE   CHARLES ADAMS PLATT   *Two Views of the Garden*

"TIMBERLINE"   W. HINKLE SMITH   BRYN MAWR, PENNSYLVANIA   CHARLES ADAMS PLATT   *Left: Entrance; Right: Garden House*

"TIMBERLINE"   W. HINKLE SMITH   BRYN MAWR, PENNSYLVANIA   CHARLES ADAMS PLATT   *Terrace Steps*

"FAULKNER FARM"   CHARLES SPRAGUE   BROOKLINE, MASSACHUSETTS   LITTLE & BROWNE   *Front Facade*

"FAULKNER FARM"   CHARLES SPRAGUE   BROOKLINE, MASSACHUSETTS   LITTLE & BROWNE   *View of Garden and Casino*

"FAULKNER FARM"   CHARLES SPRAGUE   BROOKLINE, MASSACHUSETTS   LITTLE & BROWNE   *Garden from the Casino*

"FAULKNER FARM"   CHARLES SPRAGUE   BROOKLINE, MASSACHUSETTS   LITTLE & BROWNE   *Casino Pergola Detail*

"FAULKNER FARM"   CHARLES SPRAGUE   BROOKLINE, MASSACHUSETTS   LITTLE & BROWNE   *Pool*

"FAULKNER FARM"   CHARLES SPRAGUE   BROOKLINE, MASSACHUSETTS   LITTLE & BROWNE   *Views of Pergola Walks*

"FAULKNER FARM   CHARLES SPRAGUE   BROOKLINE, MASSACHUSETTS   LITTLE & BROWNE   *Casino Facade*

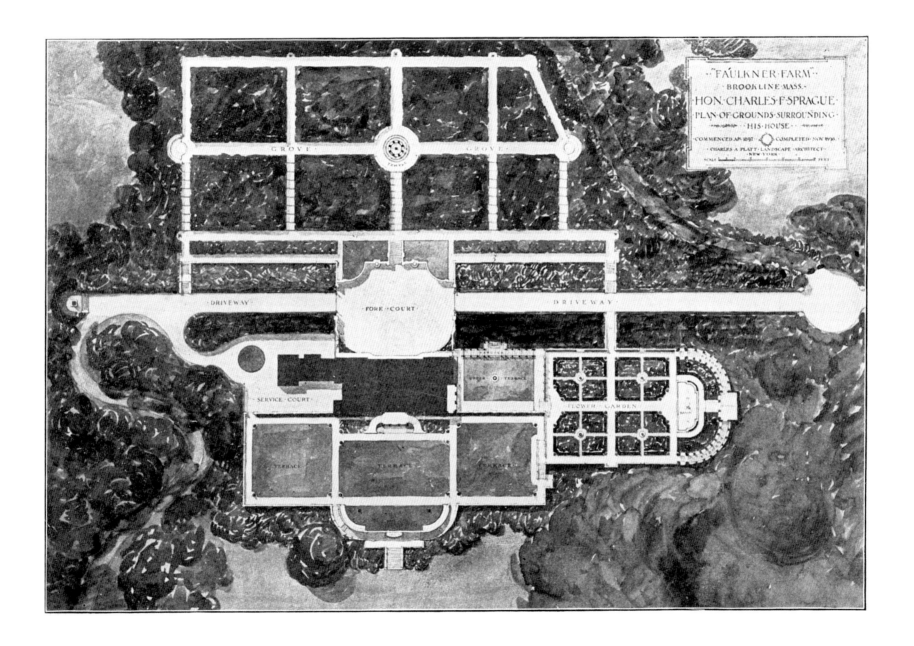

"FAULKNER FARM"   CHARLES SPRAGUE   BROOKLINE, MASSACHUSETTS   LITTLE & BROWNE   *Plan*

"JERICHO FARMS"   MIDDLETON S. BURRILL   JERICHO, NEW YORK   JOHN RUSSELL POPE   *Aerial View*

ESTATE OF ANDREW STOUT   RED BANK, NEW JERSEY   JOHN RUSSELL POPE   *Pool*

"CHETWODE"   W. STORRS WELLS   NEWPORT, RHODE ISLAND   HORACE TRUMBAUER   *Formal Garden Detail*

"CHETWODE"   W. STORRS WELLS   NEWPORT, RHODE ISLAND   HORACE TRUMBAUER   *Pool*

"CHETWODE" W. STORRS WELLS NEWPORT, RHODE ISLAND HORACE TRUMBAUER *Formal Garden View*

"GEORGIAN COURT"   GEORGE JAY GOULD   LAKEWOOD, NEW JERSEY   BRUCE PRICE   *Garden View*

"GEORGIAN COURT"   GEORGE JAY GOULD   LAKEWOOD, NEW JERSEY   BRUCE PRICE   *Bridge and Basin*

"GEORGIAN COURT"   GEORGE JAY GOULD   LAKEWOOD, NEW JERSEY   BRUCE PRICE   *Terrace and Fountain*

"GEORGIAN COURT"   GEORGE JAY GOULD   LAKEWOOD, NEW JERSEY   BRUCE PRICE   *Wellhead*

"GEORGIAN COURT"   GEORGE JAY GOULD   LAKEWOOD, NEW JERSEY   BRUCE PRICE   *Fountain*

"GEORGIAN COURT"   GEORGE JAY GOULD   LAKEWOOD, NEW JERSEY   BRUCE PRICE   *Electrical Fountain*

"ASPET"   AUGUSTUS SAINT-GAUDENS   CORNISH, NEW HAMPSHIRE   *Fountain Basin*

"ASPET"   AUGUSTUS SAINT-GAUDENS   CORNISH, NEW HAMPSHIRE   *Left: Seat in the Lily Garden; Right: Lily Garden*

ESTATE OF WALTER WATSON   ROSLYN, NEW YORK   *Terrace*

"REYNOLDA"   MRS. R. J. REYNOLDS   WINSTON-SALEM, NORTH CAROLINA   CHARLES BARTON KEEN   *Walk to Forecourt*

"REYNOLDA"   MRS. R. J. REYNOLDS   WINSTON-SALEM, NORTH CAROLINA   CHARLES BARTON KEEN   *Sunken Garden*

"CASTLE HILL"   R. T. CRANE   IPSWICH, MASSACHUSETTS   PEABODY & STEARNS   *Pergola*

"CASTLE HILL"   R. T. CRANE   IPSWICH, MASSACHUSETTS   PEABODY & STEARNS   *Grand Allée*

"CASTLE HILL"   R. T. CRANE   IPSWICH, MASSACHUSETTS   PEABODY & STEARNS   *Rose Garden*

ESTATE OF S. FULLERTON WEAVER   EAST HAMPTON, NEW YORK   SCHULTZE & WEAVER   *Swimming Pool*

ESTATE OF ETHAN ALLEN   NORTH ANDOVER, MASSACHUSETTS   *Hemlock Garden*

"NAUMKEAG"   JOSEPH H. CHOATE   STOCKBRIDGE, MASSACHUSETTS   STANFORD WHITE   *Afternoon Garden*

UNKNOWN *Swimming Pool*

ESTATE OF JOHN T. HOLLIS   HINGHAM, MASSACHUSETTS   *Garden Walk and Stone Gates*

ESTATE OF GEORGE S. PARKER   PETERSBOROUGH, NEW HAMPSHIRE   *Alpine Garden*

ESTATE OF ARTHUR V. DAVIS   MILL NECK, NEW YORK   GUY LOWELL   *Swimming Pool*

ESTATE OF LANDON K. THORNE   BAY SHORE, NEW YORK   WILLIAM F. DOMINICK   *Boat Landing*

"ROSEMARY"   J. F. CARLISLE   ISLIP, NEW YORK   TROWBRIDGE & ACKERMAN   *Aerial View*

"ROSEMARY"   J. F. CARLISLE   ISLIP, NEW YORK   TROWBRIDGE & ACKERMAN   *Left: Garden Gate; Right: Stair to Courtyard*

"CHERRYWOOD"   JOHN VIETOR   LOCUST VALLEY, NEW YORK   JAMES W. O'CONNOR   *Cedar Allée*

"ANNANDALE FARM"   MOSES TAYLOR   MT. KISCO, NEW YORK   *Formal Garden*

"ANNANDALE FARM"   MOSES TAYLOR   MT. KISCO, NEW YORK   *Pergola*

"ANNANDALE FARM" MOSES TAYLOR MT. KISCO, NEW YORK *Terrace*

"THE ORCHARD"   JAMES LAWRENCE BREESE   SOUTHAMPTON, NEW YORK   McKIM, MEAD & WHITE   *Garden Facade*

"THE ORCHARD"   JAMES LAWRENCE BREESE   SOUTHAMPTON, NEW YORK   McKIM, MEAD & WHITE   *Pergola*

"THE ORCHARD"   JAMES LAWRENCE BREESE   SOUTHAMPTON, NEW YORK   McKIM, MEAD & WHITE   *The Garden*

"WOODLAND"   HENRY W. POOR   TUXEDO, NEW YORK   T. HENRY RANDALL   *Garden Facade*

"WOODLAND"   HENRY W. POOR   TUXEDO, NEW YORK   T. HENRY RANDALL   *Garden and Terrace*

"BOX HILL"   STANFORD WHITE   ST. JAMES, NEW YORK   McKIM, MEAD & WHITE   *Garden Facade*

"BOX HILL"   STANFORD WHITE   ST. JAMES, NEW YORK   McKIM, MEAD & WHITE   *Driveway*

"BOX HILL"   STANFORD WHITE   ST. JAMES, NEW YORK   McKIM, MEAD & WHITE   *Garden View*

"BOX HILL"   STANFORD WHITE   ST. JAMES, NEW YORK   McKIM, MEAD & WHITE   *Pergola*

Landscape Architect Biographies

ALBRO & LINDEBERG

Lewis Colt Albro (1876–1924) and Harrie T. Lindeberg (1879–1959) were both trained in the offices of McKim, Mead & White prior to opening their own architectural office in 1906, and they remained partners until 1914. The firm of Albro & Lindeberg specialized in domestic architecture; their James Stillman residence at Pocantico Hills, New York, and Foxhollow Farm at Rhinebeck, New York, established them as masters of country house design. Following the dissolution of the firm, both Albro and Lindeberg practiced independently. Albro produced works that were generally more classically inspired, and Lindeberg creating designs that were distinctly romantic in nature, even slightly idiosyncratic with their deftly handled yet disparate design elements. The landscape design of the former partners' various separate projects further illustrates these opposing approaches.

CHESTER H. ALDRICH

See Delano & Aldrich

MABEL KEYES BABCOCK

Author, educator, and landscape architect, Mabel Keyes Babcock (1861–1931) received an M.S. from MIT in 1909 and practiced primarily in Boston and its suburbs. She taught horticulture and landscape design at Wellesley College from 1910 to 1914 and in 1918 was director of landscape at the Lowthorpe School of Landscape Architecture and Horticulture for Women, which had been founded by another woman pioneer in landscape design, Mrs. Edward G. Low. Babcock's works included the president's garden at MIT, the landscaping of Boston's Arlington Street Church, and sections of the Wellesley and Bates college campuses. At the time of her death, she was a member of President Hoover's Conference on Home Building and Ownership.

NATHAN FRANKLIN BARRETT

A Civil War veteran, Nathan Barrett (1845–1919) received his initial instruction in landscape design from the Irish itinerant gardener on his father's estate. As a result of early work on suburban station grounds for the New Jersey Central Railroad, he became associated with George Pullman and architect S. S. Beman in the creation of Pullman, Illinois, the nation's first planned industrial community. Subsequent town planning projects by Barrett included those for Chevy Chase, Maryland; Fort Worth, Texas; Birmingham, Alabama; and Rochelle Park at New Rochelle, New York. Barrett also served as landscape architect for the Essex County (New Jersey) Park Commission and the Palisades Interstate Parkway Commission for New Jersey and New York. Among his numerous residential works were commissions for the P. A. B. Widener estate in Elkins Park, Pennsylvania; H. O. Havemeyer's property at Islip, New York; and the Stockbridge, Massachusetts, summer house of Joseph H. Choate. Barrett was a founder and early president of the American Society of Landscape Architects.

HAROLD HILL BLOSSOM

A longtime employee of the Olmsted firm, Harold Hill Blossom (1879–1935) supervised its West Coast offices, overseeing the landscaping of San Diego's Balboa Park and San Francisco's Golden Gate Recreation Area. After World War I, he established an independent practice in Boston, designing landscapes in the Olmsteds' pastoral tradition at Brookline, along Boston's North Shore, and at Providence and Newport, Rhode Island. Blossom was the author of *The Landscape Beautiful* (1923).

WILLIAM WELLES BOSWORTH

Beaux-Arts-trained architect W. Welles Bosworth (1869–1966) was renowned for his corporate and institutional designs, which included the Cunard, AT&T, and Bank of New York buildings in New York City. He was equally well-known as a landscape architect and planned the campus and buildings of the MIT, the campus of Stanford University, and Arlington Cemetery. He executed numerous house and garden designs for estates outside New York City, including Kykuit, John D. Rockefeller's 5,000-acre estate at Pocantico Hills, New York; and, in collaboration with Charles W. Leavitt, the classically embellished gardens of Greystone, the Yonkers, New York, house of lawyer Samuel Untermyer. Greystone is a public park today.

Educated at MIT and the Ecole des Beaux-Arts, Bosworth worked in the offices of Carrère & Hastings, where he collaborated on the plan and landscaping of Buffalo's Pan-American Exposition, prior to establishing his own practice. During the 1920s, Bosworth spent increasing amounts of time in France, overseeing the Rockefeller-financed restoration of the Palaces of Versailles and Fontainebleau, and the cathedral at Rheims. Except during World War II, he remained a French resident until his death at age 97.

ERNEST W. BOWDITCH

A native of Brookline, Massachusetts, Ernest W. Bowditch (1850–1918) attended MIT briefly before taking construction survey jobs with the Chicago, Burlington & Quincy Railroad and the Darien Expedition seeking a route for the proposed Panama Canal. He returned to Boston and joined an engineering firm charged with the maintenance and ongoing design of the Mount Auburn Cemetery. After opening his own office in 1871, he collaborated with landscape designers Robert M. Copeland and the Olmsteds, and architects such as Peabody & Stearns, Richard Morris Hunt, and Horace Trumbauer, on the Lorillard, Vanderbilt, Goelet, and Berwind estates at Newport, Rhode Island, and the Sonnenberg Gardens at Canandaigua, New York. He proved equally adept at romantic picturesque and formal Beaux-Arts approaches to landscape design.

Bowditch's nonresidential designs included the Rockefeller and Shaker Lakes Parks in Cleveland, Ohio, and subdivisions such as Tuxedo Park, New York; Allston Park, Massachusetts; Shoreby Hill at Jamestown, Rhode Island; and Cleveland, Ohio's Clifton Park and Euclid Heights. Bowditch's papers are preserved at the Essex Institute, Salem, Massachusetts.

ARTHUR F. BRINCKERHOF

A 1902 graduate of Cornell University, A. F. Brinckerhoff (1880–1959) joined the landscape firm of Ferruccio Vitale in 1908 and was a partner from

1917 to 1924. In independent practice he fashioned landscape treatments for several estates, schools, and other institutions in and around New York City. On Long Island he designed the grounds for Greentree, the John Hay Whitney estate at Manhasset. An officer of the Fine Arts Federation of New York, the Municipal Arts Society, and the American Society of Landscape Architects, he helped shape the plans of numerous New York City parks and housing projects and served as consultant to the board of design of the 1939 New York World's Fair.

BRINLEY & HOLBROOK

Active during the first third of the 20th century, the Morristown, New Jersey, firm of Brinley & Holbrook landscaped a number of country estates in northern New Jersey and Long Island, most notably Cedar Court, the Morristown estate of Otto Kahn. On Long Island, the firm designed Winfield Hall, the F. W. Woolworth estate at Glen Cove, in collaboration with architect C. P. H. Gilbert. Brinley & Holbrook's later, nonresidential work included the grounds of the Annandale Prison Farm and New Jersey State Soldiers Home, and the campus of the State Normal School at Trenton, now the College of New Jersey.

JAMES BUSH-BROWN

Born in Newburgh, New York, James Bush-Brown (1907–1986) graduated from the University of Pennsylvania and studied at Harvard. With his wife Louise, he was the author of the noted 1939 *America's Garden Book*, which was revised in several editions and covered every phase of creating a garden including plant culture, and the care of lawns, shrubs and trees. He retired

in 1958 from his position as professor of landscape architecture and horticulture at the Pennsylvania School of Horticulture, now associated with Temple University. He also illustrated his wife's book *Young America's Garden Book* (1962).

CARRÈRE & HASTINGS

Celebrated for their design of the New York Public Library and countless other monumental urban buildings in New York City and Washington, D.C. and elsewhere, architects John Merven Carrère (1858–1911) and Thomas Hastings (1860–1929) also fashioned house and landscaping designs for a number of Beaux-Arts-style country estates in Long Island, the Hudson River Valley, Greenwich, Connecticut, and New Jersey's northern suburbs, as well as the resort communities of Newport, Rhode Island, Lenox, Massachusetts, and Elberon, New Jersey. In New York City, they designed St. Johns and Hudson parks, as well as unexecuted schemes for Bryant Park and embellishments to Central Park.

NOEL CHAMBERLIN

A member of a distinguished Boston family, Noel Chamberlin (1880?–1943) graduated from MIT in 1902 and served for a number of years as the chief landscape architect in the office of Charles W. Leavitt. In this capacity, he planned and developed the extensive landscaping at Immergrun, the estate of steel executive Charles M. Schwab at Loretto, Pennsylvania. Opening his own office in 1923, he created the landscape design for the Daniel Guggenheim estate at Sands Point, Long Island; for Rufus W. Scott at Locust Valley, Long Island; and for Robert H. Montgomery at Greenwich,

Connecticut. He also served as consultant on the Fairchild Tropical Gardens in Florida. Chamberlin was one of the three members of the selection committee for P. H. Elwood's book *American Landscape Architecture*.

OGDEN CODMAN

Coauthor with Edith Wharton of the influential book *The Decoration of Houses*, Ogden Codman (1863–1951) pursued a multifaceted career as writer–critic, antiquarian, and designer. Trained as a special student at MIT, and in the offices of Boston architects Andrews, Jacques & Rantoul, he opened offices of his own in 1891, prospering as an interior decorator while continuing his extensive study and documentation of American Colonial architecture and the chateaux of France. Less known as a landscape designer, he nonetheless created gardens and plans for the estates of Grant Schley, in Far Hills, New Jersey; M. M. Ludlow, at Oakdale, New York; Edith Wharton and J. J. Van Alen, at Newport, Rhode Island; for the Codman family house at Lincoln, Massachusetts; and his own Chateau de Grégy, southwest of Paris.

MARIAN COFFIN

One of the first prominent women landscape architects, Marian Cruger Coffin (1876–1957) completed the landscape architecture program at MIT in 1904 and received further training from Boston architect Guy Lowell before opening her own office in New York. Her first major client was former fellow MIT student Henry Francis DuPont, who was instrumental in obtaining for her the commission to design the gardens of the Rodney Sharp estate at Wilmington, Delaware. Later DuPont–related commissions included designs for several of Henry DuPont's siblings, as well as for his summer home at Southampton and the extensive grounds of Winterthur. DuPont's influence also brought Coffin work on the campus of the University of Delaware. On New York's Long Island, Coffin fashioned gardens on the Childs Frick estate at Roslyn; for Charles Sabin at Southampton; at Edward F. Hutton and Marjorie Merriweather Post's Hillwood in Wheatley Hills; and at Marshall Field's Caumsett in Lloyds Neck. Her nonresidential work included several designs for the New York Botanical Garden. Overall, Coffin designed over four dozen estates along the East Coast of the United States.

Coffin consistently championed the cause of the professional woman, employing many as apprentices in her office, several of whom became prominent designers in their own right. Elected a fellow of the American Society of Landscape Architects in 1918, she received the society's gold medal in 1930. She was also the author of *Trees and Shrubs for Landscape Effect* (1940).

RUTH BRAMLEY DEAN

Following two years at the University of Chicago and an apprenticeship in the offices of landscape architect Jens Jensen, Ruth Dean (1889–1932) opened an office in New York in 1915. After her 1923 marriage to architect Aymar Embury II, she divided her career between landscape work and writing articles for magazines including *House & Garden, House Beautiful, Country Life,* and *Garden.* By the late 1920s she was garden editor for *The Delineator.* She authored *The Livable House: Its Garden* (1917), and in 1929 she was awarded the Architectural League of New York's gold medal.

DELANO & ALDRICH

Trained at Columbia University and the Ecole des Beaux-Arts, William

Adams Delano (1874–1960) and Chester H. Aldrich (1871–1940) worked together at the offices of Carrère & Hastings prior to forming their architectural partnership in 1903. Although they were thoroughly schooled in the formal garden design traditions of the French Ecole, their numerous Long Island residential projects were often executed in collaboration with landscape architects including Beatrix Farrand, Annette Hoyt Flanders, the Olmsted Brothers, and Ferruccio Vitale. Versatile residential designers, Aldrich & Delano were equally skilled in their handling of Georgian Colonial, Federal, 18th-century French, Italian Renaissance, and, somewhat surprisingly, the Arts and Crafts style of Voysey and Lutyens. In later years, they proved equally adept at streamlined Art Moderne. In addition to their well-known country residences for J. A. Burden, Otto Kahn, Gertrude Vanderbilt Whitney, and Bertram G. Work, they created several urbane New York City town houses and clubs, along with apartment houses, office buildings, and airports. They also designed academic buildings for Yale, Smith College, and the Lawrenceville School.

CHARLES ELIOT

See Frederick Law Olmsted & Co.; Olmsted, Olmsted & Eliot;
Olmsted Brothers

PHILIP HOMER ELWOOD JR.

Best known for his comprehensive 1924 work *American Landscape Architecture,* Philip H. Elwood Jr. (1884–1960) received a B.S.A. from Cornell University in 1910. For three years he worked in the offices of Charles Leavitt before joining the agricultural faculty at Massachusetts State

College. In 1915 he moved to Columbus, Ohio, to supervise the landscaping of Ohio State University. After service in World War I, he designed the Argonne Cemetery of the American Expeditionary Forces. He returned to Columbus and joined the firm of Elwood & Frye. In 1923 he established the landscape architecture program at Iowa State University, where he taught until 1952. In addition to his work for the Ohio and Iowa State campuses, Elwood designed the landscaping for Boys Town, near Omaha, Nebraska, and created the master plan for Cañon City, Colorado.

WILSON EYRE

A master at the integration of house and landscape design, Wilson Eyre (1858–1944) was among the most influential and highly regarded residential architects of his era. Born in Italy and educated at boarding schools in the United States and Canada, he attended MIT for a single year prior to joining the offices of Philadelphia architect James Peacock Sims in 1877. Succeeding to Sims' practice five years later, he undertook the design of hundreds of country residences in and around Philadelphia, as well as Long Island, Connecticut, Massachusetts, and Rhode Island. Although clearly influenced by the residential work of English architects, such as Philip Webb and Richard Norman Shaw, Eyre developed a style of house and garden design distinctively his own. He was equally skilled as a renderer, and his architectural works were widely publicized in the architectural press and in *House & Garden* magazine, of which he was a cofounder and editor. As president of the Philadelphia chapter of the AIA, a founder of the T-Square Club, and an instructor at the University of Pennsylvania, he was a continuing advocate of design education. In 1911, with offices in both Philadelphia and New York, he established a partnership with John G. McIlvaine. The firm of Eyre & McIlvaine endured until 1939.

BEATRIX JONES FARRAND

A true pioneer in landscape architecture, Beatrix Jones Farrand (1872–1959) overcame prejudice and the dismissive attitudes of her peers towards professional women through her distinguished achievements as a designer. Farrand was the only woman among the founders of the American Society of Landscape Architects, and she helped make possible the careers of many gifted women landscape designers. The daughter of a distinguished New York family and the niece of Edith Wharton, Farrand studied landscape design with Charles Sprague Sargent, director of the Arnold Arboretum at Cambridge, Massachusetts. Her numerous residential projects in the United States and England include the grounds of Dumbarton Oaks at Washington, D.C., the Westbury, New York, estate of Willard D. Straight, and John D. Rockefeller's summer residence at Seal Harbor, Maine. She supervised or consulted on the landscaping of the campuses of Princeton and Yale universities; the University of Chicago; Hamilton, Oberlin, Occidental, and Vassar colleges; the Arnold Arboretum; and the Santa Barbara Botanic Garden. Beatrix Farrand's archives are held by the University of California at Berkeley and by Dumbarton Oaks.

ANNETTE HOYT FLANDERS

A native of Milwaukee, Wisconsin, Annette Hoyt Flanders (1889–1946) received her education from Smith College, the University of Illinois, the Marquette University School of Engineering, and the Sorbonne. She joined the firm of Vitale, Brinckerhoff & Geifert circa 1919, became an associate in 1921, and in the following year established her own practice. She designed numerous residential landscapes on Long Island, most notably the Vincent Astor estate at Port Washington and the Charles E. F. McCann estate at Oyster Bay, for which she was awarded the Architectural League's gold medal. Flanders returned in the late 1930s to Milwaukee, where she established a new office and continued to design gardens in the Midwest and Southwest, and as far afield as Hawaii. Her distinctive "classic modern" approach to landscape architecture was represented at Chicago's 1933 Century of Progress Exposition.

BRYANT FLEMING

A native of Buffalo, New York, Bryant Fleming (1877–1946) pursued a specially devised program in horticulture and architectural design at Cornell University under the eminent naturalist Liberty Hyde Bailey. Following graduation, he spent three years in the Boston office of Warren Manning before returning to Cornell in 1904 to join Bailey in the establishment of the Department of Landscape Art in Cornell University's College of Agriculture. Fleming served as the department's director from 1906 to 1915.

In 1905, Fleming established a design practice with Frederick Townsend in Buffalo, and they created landscaping and subdivision plans for residences throughout the Midwest, most notably the Frank Lloyd Wright–designed Coonley estate in Riverside, Illinois. In 1915 Fleming went into practice on his own, designing residential landscapes throughout the East from Florida to southern Canada. In 1925, Cornell appointed him university landscape advisor, and he moved his extensive practice to Ithaca, New

York. Notable in this period was his design of Belle Meade, a residential suburb of Nashville, Tennessee. As a longtime educator at Cornell, Fleming trained a substantial generation of landscape architects.

CLARENCE FOWLER

A prominent New York landscape architect and president of the New York chapter of the American Society of Landscape Architects, Clarence Fowler (1870–1935) developed large estates for Winthrop W. Aldrich, Walter P. Bliss, George St. George, Paul Stuyvesant, and Spencer Weed, and, during a brief partnership with Ferruccio Vitale, several members of the du Pont family at Wilmington, Delaware. He also landscaped the grounds of the Quaker Ridge Golf Club in Mamaroneck, New York. Educated at Exeter Academy and Harvard University's School of Landscape Architecture, he was first employed by the Boston firm of H. Langford Warren and his commission to landscape the Fort Monroe (Virginia) military base helped establish his independent practice. During his years as an officer of the ASLA, he served as a public spokesman for the development of the Central Park Mall and the improvement of the city's other parks and squares. He also served as the chairman of New York's City Club committee on parks and playgrounds.

ROBERT LUDLOW FOWLER JR.

Following two years at Harvard University's School of Landscape Architecture, Robert L. Fowler Jr. (1887–1973) opened a practice in New York. Working closely with McKim, Mead & White, Delano & Aldrich, Mott Schmidt, and other architects, Fowler produced a host of landscape designs for country houses throughout Long Island, the Hudson Valley, and Connecticut

from the 1920s to the 1950s. His best-known nonresidential design was the landscaping of the headquarters of Reader's Digest, in Pleasantville, New York.

ISABELLA STEWART GARDNER

Isabella Stewart Gardner (1840–1924) was an influential art collector whose Italian villa on Boston's Fenway was a center of Boston culture. Born into a wealthy New York family, she married the Bostonian John L. Gardner Jr. and shocked the insular world of aristocratic Boston with her friendships and active social life. A friend of Henry James, John Singer Sargent, Elsie de Wolfe, Paul Manship, Henry Adams, and Bernard Berenson, Gardner was dedicated to her garden at Green Hill, the Brookline estate she and her husband inherited from John L. Gardner, Sr.

CHARLES FREEMAN GILLETTE

A renowned exponent of traditional Colonial garden design, Charles F. Gillette (1886–1969) trained in the office of Warren Manning before establishing his own firm in 1914 at Richmond, Virginia. Prominent among his early works were the gardens of the historic Nelson House at Yorktown and Kenmore, the Mary Washington house at Fredericksburg. In the 1920s and 1930s he created the landscaping for Virginia House and Agecroft, two reconstructed English manor houses at Windsor Farms, Virginia, and numerous other residential commissions in Virginia and North Carolina. During the 1950s, he relandscaped the grounds of the Virginia Governor's Mansion and created the early corporate campuses of the Reynolds Metals and Ethyl Companies. Gillette's papers and photographs of his work are preserved at the State Library of Virginia, and his achievements as a landscape architect are the subject of

George C. Longest's book *Genius in the Garden: Charles F. Gillette and Landscape Architecture in Virginia* (1992).

JACQUES AUGUSTE HENRI GRÉBER

The son of French sculptor Henri Gréber, Jacques Gréber (1882–1962) graduated from the Ecole des Beaux-Arts in 1908 and came to the United States to work for Clarence H. Mackay at his estate, Harbor Hill, in Roslyn, New York. He collaborated with Horace Trumbauer on numerous projects, including the Elkins Park, Pennsylvania, gardens of Joseph E. Widener's Lynnewood Hall and Edward T. Stotesbury's Whitemarsh Hall in Wyndmoor, Pennsylvania. A skilled classicist who adapted French and English traditions to the American terrain, Gréber was a noted urban planner, and worked on commissions for Ottawa and Philadelphia. He was the chief architect for the 1937 International Paris Exposition.

JAMES L. GREENLEAF

A native of New York's Catskill Mountains region, James L. Greenleaf (1857–1933) graduated from Columbia University's School of Mines in 1880. He taught there as an instructor and adjunct professor until 1894, when he opened his own civil engineering office. Increasingly, he became involved with landscape architecture, designing the grounds of some 30 country estates between 1910 and 1920. Among the most prominent of these were his projects for James B. Duke at Somerville, New Jersey; the Italian garden at Frederick W. Vanderbilt's estate at Hyde Park, New York; Blairsden, the C. Ledyard Blair estate at Peapack, New Jersey; and Killenworth, the estate of George D. Pratt at Glen Cove, Long Island.

During the 1920s, Greenleaf served on the National Commission of Fine Arts, developing landscape plans for numerous sites in Washington, D.C., and advising the Department of the Interior on the treatment of national parks. He served as national president of the American Society of Landscape Architects, as well as its New York chapter, and he was a vice president of the Architectural League of New York and recipient of its 1921 landscaping medal. He devoted much of his later years to landscape painting.

HARE & HARE

Sidney J. Hare (1860–1938) and S. Herbert Hare (1888–1960), father and son, were esteemed for their many park, subdivision, and cemetery designs. Their Kansas City firm is best known for its planning of developer J. C. Nichols' Country Club Plaza and District, particularly its residential estate component, Mission Hills. Working with city planner George Kessler, the firm helped design Kansas City's boulevard and park system and the town of Longview, Washington. On their own, they completed the grounds of the Nelson Gallery of Art and several of Missouri's state parks. Their campus landscapes included work for the University of Kansas at Lawrence, the University of Texas at Austin, and the University of Houston. The elder Hare received his landscape training from Kessler while both were employed by the Kansas City city engineer's office during the 1880s and 1890s. The younger Hare studied landscape planning at Harvard University under Frederick Law Olmsted Sr.

THOMAS HASTINGS
See Carrère & Hastings

M. H. HORVATH

Little is known concerning the landscape architect M. H. Horvath. He was active in the first decade of the 20th century in northeastern Ohio, with offices in the Citizens Bank Building in Cleveland. Correspondence between Horvath and Lucy Eliot Keeler may indicate his involvement with the landscaping of the Rutherford B. Hayes Memorial.

LOUISE HUBBARD

Chicago North Shore–based landscape architect Louise Hubbard (1887–1932) is best known for her work on the Lake Forest, Illinois, estate of Albert Lasker, on which she collaborated with architect David Adler. Following the onset of illness and her later death at age 45, her designs for the Lasker property were completed by James L. Greenleaf.

HORATIO HOLLIS HUNNEWELL

A wealthy railroad executive and financier, H. H. Hunnewell (1810–1902) is remembered today as a philanthropist and dedicated amateur botanist. He began developing what is now the Hunnewell Arboretum, on his country estate Wellesley, in the 1840s. Inspired by Italian gardens of the Renaissance, Hunnewell's pioneering efforts in landscaping introduced a number of foreign plant species to America, including many European varieties of evergreen and the rhododendron.

The creation of the conifer collection at Boston's Arnold Arboretum also came about through his efforts. Hunnewell's philanthropic endeavors included assuring the survival of the Arboretum under the auspices of Wellesley College—both the town and college took the name of Hunnewell's

estate—and financial gifts to botanist Asa Gray for the completion of his work *Flora of North America*.

INNOCENTI & WEBEL

Umberto Innocenti (1895–1968) came to America from his native Italy in 1925 after studying at the University of Florence. He worked in the office of Ferruccio Vitale and Alfred Geiffret Jr. where he became their primary project supervisor. In 1931 he left the firm and with Harvard-educated Richard K. Webel (1900–2000) formed the partnership of Innocenti & Webel in Roslyn, New York. The partnership endured until Innocenti's death, and the firm continues to this day. With Webel as the draftsman and designer dedicated to landscape theory and Innocenti as the horticulturalist who could not draw but who had a deep understanding of plant cultivation, their firm pioneered the concept of "final planting." Working with nurseries including Lewis & Valentine, mature trees and developed under-story planting were cultivated and installed to create garden landscapes that appeared long established. The firm executed notable residential projects including the estates of Landon K. Thorne, Howard K. Phipps, and Childs Frick, as well as landscapes for the Readers Digest Headquarters in Pleasantville, New York, the Greenbrier Hotel in White Sulphur Springs, and for development projects in Hobe Sound and Jupiter Island, Florida.

JENS JENSEN

Among the most admired and influential landscape architects of the 20th century, Jens Jensen (1860–1951) was born in Denmark and immigrated to the United States in 1884. His first employment was as a laborer on a Florida celery plantation. He moved to Chicago, where he worked for the city's parks department. Jensen created his first park design in 1888, and he served as superintendent and supervising architect for Chicago's park system from 1906 to 1920, developing the city's Columbus, Humboldt, and Garfield parks, as well as several smaller projects. In 1920 he went into private practice, creating landscape designs for both the Henry and Edsel Ford estates near Detroit, the Henry Ford Museum, and the Julius Rosenwald and Ogden Armour estates. Jensen was a pioneer in Prairie School landscape design, and used indigenous plants, including weeds and wild flowers in plans that reflected the native landscape of his projects. His architectural collaborators included Louis Sullivan, Frank Lloyd Wright, and Albert Kahn. In 1935, Jensen established The Clearing, a school of art at Ellison Bay, Wisconsin, and taught there until his death. He authored numerous articles and books, including *Siftings* (1939) and *The Clearing* (1949).

KEEN & MEAD

One of the first graduates of the architectural program at the University of Pennsylvania, Charles Barton Keen (1868–1931) entered the office of Philadelphia architect Frank Miles Day as a draftsman in 1890. Four years later, he established independent practice in partnership with fellow Day employee Frank Mead, pioneering the design of houses and gardens in the Pennsylvania Colonial tradition.

Keen practiced alone after Mead's 1901 departure for Cleveland, and his work grew exponentially with residential projects in Philadelphia's suburbs, New Jersey shore communities, and, in association with the Woodmere Land Association, Long Island's Five Towns region. He ultimately compiled a list of commissions that spread from Maine to Florida. Increasing patronage from the Reynolds and Duke families of North Carolina led him to move his principal offices to Winston-Salem in 1923. Throughout his long and prolific career, Keen's house and garden designs continued to be in the regional vernacular tradition.

DANIEL W. LANGTON

Daniel W. Langton (1859–1909) was one of the 11 founders of the American Society of Landscape Architects in 1899. His career consisted largely of residential work in northern New Jersey and New York's Hudson Valley, perhaps the best known of which was his design for the gardens and grounds of Drumthwacket in Princeton, now the official residence of New Jersey's governor. In collaboration with fellow ASLA founder Charles N. Lowrie, Langton is also credited with the 1907 design of West Side Park (now Lincoln Park) at Hoboken, New Jersey. An apostle of the City Beautiful movement, he maintained offices in New York City and a home in Morristown, New Jersey. He committed suicide in 1909 at age 50.

CHARLES DOWNING LAY

A native of Newburgh, New York, Charles Downing Lay (1877–1956) joined the office of Daniel W. Langton after graduating from Columbia University's School of Architecture in 1900 and the landscape design program at Harvard University in 1902. In 1904 he established his own practice, which endured until 1948. In addition to residential projects, town and subdivision plans, and park designs in New York and Connecticut, Lay served as landscape architect for the New York City Parks Department. The author of numerous magazine pieces and two books, Lay was the founder of *Landscape Architecture* and its editor from 1910 to 1920.

CHARLES WELLFORD LEAVITT

Preferring to call himself a landscape engineer rather than an architect, Charles Leavitt (1871–1928) gained experience as a civil engineer working on railroads, water systems, and infrastructure planning before commencing work as a landscaper in 1897. He created both public and private projects, and his country estate plans included those for Charles M. Schwab at Loretto, Pennsylvania; George B. Post at Bernardsville, New Jersey; John F. Dodge at Grosse Pointe, Michigan; Foxhall Keene at Westbury, New York; and, in collaboration with architect Welles Bosworth, the grounds of Greystone, the Untermyer property at Yonkers, New York. Leavitt's civic and public work was prodigious. He created: city plans for Garden City and Long Beach, New York, Cape May, New Jersey, and Lakeland, Florida; park designs for Camden, New Jersey; Philadelphia, Pennsylvania, and Colorado Springs, Colorado; engineering design of the Palisades Interstate Parkway and Storm King Highway; campus plans for the Universities of Georgia and South Carolina, and Lehigh University at Bethlehem, Pennsylvania; numerous golf courses; and the Belmont and Saratoga race courses.

LEWIS & VALENTINE

Established in 1914, the firm of Lewis & Valentine was Long Island's largest nursery operation, providing shrub and tree stock to a number of the area's great estates, New York's Central Park and Roosevelt Island, the Long Island Parkway system, and private and public golf courses. During the 1920s, with clients throughout the Middle Atlantic region, the firm made a specialty of the successful transplanting of full-grown trees, transforming former farm fields into arresting arboreal enclaves. With virtually all of metropolitan New York's landscape architects numbering among their clients, Lewis & Valentine also provided design and maintenance services to Long Island's numerous country estates.

HARRIE T. LINDEBERG
See Albro & Lindeberg

LITTLE & BROWNE

Little & Browne, Boston's premier firm of residential architects, was established in 1889. Its two principals, Arthur Little (1852–1925) and Herbert W. C. Browne (1860–1946), were educated respectively at MIT and the Boston Museum of Fine Arts and served separate apprenticeships with Peabody & Stearns and Andrews, Jacques & Rantoul. Little & Browne designed in a wide range of styles, although their best-known residential work, in both house and garden designs, displayed sensitivity to and appreciation for New England's Colonial traditions. Although their works were mostly to be found along Boston's North Shore and western suburbs, they also executed projects in New York and Chicago, as well as in Washington, D.C., where the Lars Anderson residence was a notable achievement. Early advocates of preservation, Little & Browne were responsible for the restoration of Boston's Harrison Grey Otis house as headquarters for the Society for the Preservation of New England Antiquities, now known as historic New England.

WARREN HENRY MANNING

Warren Henry Manning (1860–1938) was the son of a Massachusetts nurseryman who spent his early years working in his father's business. In 1888, he left that business and entered the office of Frederick Law Olmsted Sr., where he worked for eight years, specializing in horticulture and planting design, eventually supervising over 100 projects. When it became apparent that Charles Eliot and Olmsted's sons would become the heirs to the firm, Manning went out on his own in 1896, working with his brother J. Woodward from 1901 to 1904. Early clients would prove enduring, particularly William G. Mather, for whom Manning designed the landscape of Pinehurst in North Carolina, and Mather's Cleveland house where he collaborated with Charles Platt on the estate grounds and a 21-acre wild garden. Important residential projects included the estates of Gustave Pabst in Milwaukee, Wisconsin; August and Adolphus Busch in St. Louis, Missouri; and Cyrus and Harriet McCormick in Lake Forest, Illinois. Of seemingly limitless energy, Manning worked throughout America on over 1,700 jobs ranging from the planning of mining towns in Michigan to regional mapping projects in support of the National Park Service Bill, 1915–1916. He employed many of the period's prominent landscape designers including A.D. Taylor, Fletcher Steele, Charles F. Gillette, and Wilbur D. Cook Jr.

McKIM, MEAD & WHITE

The most famed and accomplished architectural firm of their era, McKim, Mead & White—Charles H. McKim (1847–1909), William Rutherford Mead (1846–1928), and Stanford White (1853–1906)—require no further introduction here as to the scope of their achievement or influence. Their specific role as landscape architects and planners is best exemplified in their campus designs for Columbia and New York universities and their work for the University of Virginia. The landscaping of their numerous country house commissions was generally undertaken in close collaboration with leading contemporaries in the field of landscape design: Frederick Law Olmsted and his two sons, Nathan F. Barrett, and Frenchman Jacques Gréber figuring most prominently. Stanford White, prior to his 1906 murder, was the firm's partner believed to work most closely with the landscaping professionals. White is given sole credit for the landscaping of Box Hill, his country house at St. James, New York.

MELLOR, MEIGS & HOWE

The architectural firm of Mellor, Meigs & Howe, made up of Walter Mellor (1880–1940), Arthur I. Meigs (1882–1956), and George Howe (1886–1955), was greatly esteemed for its distinctive design of country and suburban residences. The architects were also well regarded for the naturalistic landscapes in which their houses were set. Although they designed a handful of fraternity houses and college clubs, their residential works were confined to Philadelphia and its suburbs. Generally serving as the sole authors of a project's landscape design, on numerous occasions Mellor, Meig & Howe collaborated with Philadelphia-based landscape architects such as Thomas W. Sears, the firm of Harrison, Mertz & Emlen, and the now forgotten Oglesby Paul. The firm of Mellor & Meigs was established in 1906; George Howe became a partner in the firm in 1917. Following Howe's departure 11 years later, the firm reverted to its original name and continued in operation until 1940.

MORRELL & NICHOLS

Anthony Urbanski Morell (1875–1924) was born and educated in France. After emigrating to the United States, he spent his early professional years in the New York office of Charles Leavitt Jr., working with another young associate, Arthur Nichols. After working together on the Chester Congdon estate in Duluth, Minnesota, the two young designers formed a partnership in 1909 and moved to Minneapolis. Morell designed city plans for Ojibwa, Wisconsin, Saskatoon, Saskatchewan, and in 1922 worked on the plans for a new Minneapolis civic center. Born in West Springfield, Massachusetts, Arthur Richardson Nichols (1880–1970) was the first graduate of the MIT landscape architecture program. After working for a year in Schenectady, New York, Nichols joined the firm of Charles Leavitt Jr., where he worked on the development of Long Beach, New York. An advocate of long views and restrained planting, Morrell worked on the formal French-inspired gardens for the Russell M. Bennett estate on Lake Minnetonka, Minnesota, and for other private properties in the region. Morell & Nichols were involved in the early development of Minnesota and the adjacent five-state region, and developed plans for residential subdivisions, parks, college campuses, parkways, and country clubs. After Morell's death, Nichols continued to work with other firms and partnerships, and helped to establish the prestigious landscape architecture program at Iowa State University.

ROSE STANDISH NICHOLS

A member of Boston's Beacon Hill society. Rose Standish Nichols (1872–1960) was a suffragette, a dedicated pacifist, and the founder in 1915 of the Woman's International League for Peace and Freedom. She supported her social activism through landscape design after being encouraged by Charles Platt to attend the first women's professional landscape program introduced by MIT in 1900. She wrote the much acclaimed *English Pleasure Gardens (1902)*, dedicated to her uncle Augustus Saint-Gaudens, with plans by Allen H. Cox, the son of Kenyon Cox. At a time when little was published on European gardens, Nichols' book and its sequels, *Spanish and Portuguese Gardens* (1924) and *Italian Pleasure Gardens* (1928), were considered essential resources for gardeners, tourists, and historians. With a special interest in native American plants, Nichols worked with the noted architects of her time, collaborating on several Lake Forest gardens with Howard Van Doren Shaw and David Adler.

FREDERICK LAW OLMSTED & CO.
OLMSTED, OLMSTED, & ELLIOT
OLMSTED BROTHERS

The veritable founding father of landscape architecture in America, Frederick Law Olmsted Sr. (1822–1903) is justly famed for his design of New York's Central Park, Brooklyn's Prospect Park, Washington's Mall, and scores of other urban and national parks, plans for residential communities, and school and college campuses. He was almost single-handedly responsible for establishing civic recognition of parks as a vital amenity to cities and a social benefit to their citizens. His landscaping of large country estates played a secondary role to the more prominent public projects, but Olmsted Sr.'s design for Biltmore, the vast Asheville, North Carolina, estate and forest preserve of George W. Vanderbilt, qualifies him as a pioneer in residential landscaping as well.

From 1857 to 1883, Olmsted's professional offices were in New York, and he practiced both independently and in collaboration with architect Calvert Vaux. In 1884, Olmsted moved his offices to Brookline, Massachusetts, where, as the principal of Frederick Law Olmsted & Company, he oversaw the creation of nearby Boston's interconnected series of parks, parkways, waterways, and arboretum, known as the "Emerald Necklace." In 1895, Olmsted's stepson, John Charles Olmsted (1852–1920), and author–landscape architect Charles Eliot (1859–1897) became partners in the firm, and its name changed to Olmsted, Olmsted & Eliot. With the retirement of the elder Olmsted and death of Charles Eliot in 1897, the youthful Frederick Law Olmsted Jr. (1870–1957) was raised to partnership and the firm renamed Olmsted Brothers. Under this name, it endured until the 1950s.

Although Olmsted Brothers continued its founder's commitment to the public park and City Beautiful movements with projects for the McMillan Plan for Washington, D.C., and master plans for Baltimore's Roland Park, New York's Forest Hills Gardens, and Los Angeles' Palos Verdes Estates, they were equally involved with residential projects, such as those for William R. Coe, Oyster Bay, New York; Walter Jennings, Cold Spring Harbor, New York; and Richard T. Crane, Jr., Ipswich, Massachusetts, to name but a few.

SAMUEL PARSONS JR.

The son of a nurseryman and a graduate of both Haverford College and Yale University's Sheffield Scientific School, landscape architect and author Samuel Parsons (1844–1923) gained practical experience in the family nursery firm prior to joining in 1879 the office of architect Calvert Vaux who had been the partner of Andrew Jackson Downing. Working with Vaux until his death in 1895, and succeeding him thereafter, during a 30-year period Parsons oversaw the design and/or creation of Central, Riverside, and Morningside parks in New York, as well as Bowling Green and Union and Abington squares. Outside New York he worked on San Diego's Balboa Park, Philadelphia's League Island Park, and the Capitol grounds at Washington. Among his designs for private clients were Inisfada, the Nicholas Brady estate at Roslyn, New York; and Elmendorf Farms, George Widener's racing stables at Lexington, Kentucky. The author of numerous magazine articles and six books on landscape architecture, Samuel Parsons was also a leading figure in establishing the American Society of Landscape Architects, drafting it constitution and serving as its second president.

CHARLES ADAMS PLATT

Initially a highly regarded landscape painter, the Paris-trained Charles Adams Platt (1861–1933) made his first forays into design with his 1894 book on Renaissance garden design, *Italian Gardens*, and a series of houses and gardens at the artists' colony of Cornish, New Hampshire. Following work at Charles F. Sprague and Lars Anderson estates at Brookline, Massachusetts (1897 and 1902), during the next two decades he gained increasing renown for his adaptation of Italian garden traditions to American landscapes in country residences he designed in New York, Connecticut, Massachusetts, Pennsylvania, Ohio, and Illinois. With no formal horticultural training, he often worked with landscape architects including the Olmsted Brothers, Ellen Biddle Shipman, and Warren Manning. During the 1920s he created master plans for the campuses of Connecticut College for Women, the University of Illinois, and, with Guy Lowell, Phillips Andover Academy. He also designed numerous urban structures for the Astor Estate in New York City and the Freer Gallery of Art at Washington, D.C. Platt attained preeminence in virtually any field he chose to enter. His landscape and architectural achievements were the first to be published as a photographic record, *Monograph of the Work of Charles Adams Platt* (1913).

JOHN RUSSELL POPE

One of the most prolific and influential residential designers of the early 20th century, John Russell Pope (1873–1937) attended the City College of New York, Columbia University, and the Ecole des Beaux-Arts prior to joining the office of architect Bruce Price in 1900. Following Price's demise in 1903, Pope established an independent practice. Pope was deeply concerned with all aspects of the proper site and surroundings of his works, which were either overseen directly by him or created in close collaboration with designers whose work he trusted and admired. Among his most frequent collaborators were the Olmsted Brothers, Ellen Biddle Shipman, and Ferruccio Vitale.

BRUCE PRICE

One of the most respected architects of the 1880s and 1890s, Bruce Price (1845–1903) was born and raised in Maryland and trained in the offices of Baltimore architects Niernsee & Neilson. Practicing independently after

1873, he established offices in New York in 1877. Price was well known for his design of early Manhattan skyscrapers as well as stations and hotels for the Canadian Pacific Railroad. His skills as a landscape designer are best exemplified by his work at Georgian Court, the Lakewood, New Jersey, estate of George Gould, and Tuxedo Park, the vast sporting and cottage complex developed by Pierre Lorillard in Orange County, New York, for which Price planned all the initial buildings and laid out the roadways and grounds.

AUGUSTA AND AUGUSTUS SAINT-GAUDENS

The Irish-born Augustus Saint-Gaudens (1848–1907) was an American sculptor associated with the Beaux-Arts movement and the American Renaissance. Educated in New York at Cooper Union and the National Academy of Design, Saint-Gaudens traveled to Europe where he studied architecture and art in the atelier of François Jouffroy at the Ecole des Beaux-Arts. Saint-Gaudens gained fame for his memorials, noted for their direct naturalism, to the heroes of the American Civil War. After being diagnosed with cancer in 1900, he moved permanently to his Cornish, New Hampshire Federal house with a barn–studio and gardens designed by the artist and his wife, Augusta Saint-Gaudens (1848–1926), an artist in her own right. Members of the Cornish community included artists Kenyon Cox, Maxfield Parrish, and George Deforest Brush; the architect Charles Adams Platt; and sculptors Paul Manship and Louis Saint-Gaudens.

RICHARD J. SCHERMERHORN JR.

Richard Schermerhorn (1878–1962) was born in Brooklyn, New York, and educated at Brooklyn and Rensselaer Polytechnic institutes. In addition to his residential projects, Schermerhorn prepared master plans for the communities of Great Neck, Huntington, and Lawrence on Long Island. He was also a consultant for New York's Allegheny and Taconic state parks, and landscape architect for the Hudson River Conservancy. He was a leading advocate of preserving parks as open space uncluttered by memorials, art and music centers, and other encroachments.

THOMAS W. SEARS

Born in Brookline, Massachusetts, and educated at Harvard University, Thomas W. Sears (1880–1960) practiced briefly in Providence, Rhode Island, before setting up an office in Philadelphia, Pennsylvania. There he collaborated with many of the city's important residential architects over a period of four decades. Chief among these were Paul Cret; Wilson Eyre; Horace Trumbauer; Zantzinger, Borie & Medary; and Charles Barton Keen, with whom Sears designed Reynolda, the R. J. Reynolds estate at Winston-Salem, North Carolina. Sears' nonresidential commissions included the grounds of the Dunwoody Home and Penn Charter School; the Washington Memorial Chapel at Valley Forge; the gardens at Pennsbury, William Penn's re-created colonial home; and Philadelphia's Washington Square and Fairmount Park. Sears' voluminous photographic record of both his own work and his extensive travels abroad is preserved at the Smithsonian Institution.

ARTHUR A. SHURTLEFF (SHURCLIFF)

The designer of public and private projects in and around Boston, Arthur Shurtleff (1870–1957) changed his name in 1930 to its early family spelling, Shurcliff. He graduated from MIT in 1894 and continued his education at Harvard University under the tutelage of Olmsted partner Charles Eliot. After joining the Olmsted firm in 1896, he worked with Eliot on the restoration of the town commons of Newburyport and Weston, Massachusetts, and Sandwich, New Hampshire. In 1899 he assisted Frederick Olmsted Jr. in establishing Harvard's landscape program. Entering independent practice in 1904, Shurtleff fashioned a number of landscape designs for country estates along Boston's North Shore, including Castle Hill, the Richard Crane property at Ipswich, and Greycourt, the Methuen estate of Charles H. Tenney. His extensive civic designs included his work with the Olmsteds on the "Emerald Necklace" plan for the Boston Fens, and the landscaping of the Charles River Basin and Storrow Drive. Among his institutional works were projects for Amherst College, Brown University, and Wellesley College, and secondary schools Deerfield, Groton, and St. Paul's. From 1928 to 1941, he was associated with architects Perry, Shaw & Hepburn on the creation of Colonial Williamsburg, including the Colonial Parkway between Williamsburg and Yorktown. He performed similar service for the restoration of Old Sturbridge Village.

FLETCHER STEELE

Raised in the rural New York community of Pittsford, Fletcher Steele (1885–1971) attended Williams College and Harvard University, where he was enrolled in the landscape program. He worked for Boston landscape architect Warren Manning prior to setting up his own office in 1914. A brilliant and innovative designer, he introduced modernist architectural and sculptural elements to his landscapes, most notably at his 1915 Rochester,

New York, garden for Charlotte Whitney; his 1920s–1930s alterations for Naumkeag, the Choate estate at Stockbridge, Massachusetts; an outdoor amphitheater for the Camden, New Jersey public library grounds; and the Worcester, Massachusetts gardens of Robert Stoddard. Steele was the author of *Design in the Little Garden* (1926).

ELIZABETH LEONARD STRANG

The daughter of an upstate New York farmer, Elizabeth Leonard Strang (1886–1948) entered the still-developing landscape architecture program at Cornell University in 1905 and graduated five years later, the first woman to complete the school's program. Following an extensive apprenticeship with designers including Ferruccio Vitale and Ellen Biddle Shipman, Strang established her own practice in Massachusetts and taught landscape design at the Lowthorpe School of Landscape Architecture and Horticulture for Women. Well remembered for the numerous articles she wrote for the popular home and garden periodicals of the era, Strang's descriptions of her work and how its was accomplished were a major stimulus to the application of landscape architecture to middle-class American suburbs rather than to large estates.

VITALE & GEIFFERT

Born in Florence, Italy, Ferruccio Vitale (1875–1933) came to the United States as a military attaché to the Italian Embassy in 1898. Schooled as an engineer and architect in his native land, he turned to landscaping through the influence of George F. Pentecost Jr., receiving training from both Pentecost and Samuel Parsons Jr. as an employee in their offices. In 1905,

when Parsons joined the New York City Parks Department, Pentecost and Vitale formed a partnership. They designed projects for the Wanamakers and Samuel Bodine in the suburbs of Philadelphia, but the firm dissolved during the financial depression of 1907–09. Independently and in brief partnerships from 1908 to 1917, Vitale designed notable formal residential installations for Brookside, the Walker estate at Great Barrington, Massachusetts; Nemours and Longwood, the country homes of Alfred and Pierre DuPont in Delaware and Pennsylvania; and for Isaac and Solomon Guggenheim at Port Washington, Long Island.

In 1917, Vitale brought employees Alfred Geiffert Jr. (1890–1957) and Arthur Brinckerhoff into partnership. Geiffert had joined Vitale as an office boy in 1908, then studied landscape design at Columbia University. Brinckerhoff departed to form his own office in 1924. From 1917 to the 1930s, Vitale & Geiffert was among the most prominent landscape architecture firms of its day, executing scores of residential commissions throughout the East and Midwest. Their prominent works are too numerous to be cited individually; mention must be made, however, of the firm's work at Allgates, in Haverford Pennsylvania; Inisfada, Roslyn, New York; the Long Island estates of Langdon Thorne and John A. Vietor; Skyland Farms, Sloatsburg, New York; and the Richard King Mellon estate, Pittsburgh, Pennsylvania. Their nonresidential commissions, although not extensive, included a master plan of Scarsdale, New York, and the south campus of the University of Illinois.

Following Vitale's death in 1933, Geiffert continued the firm's operation until 1957. In addition to his work with Vitale, Geiffert is generally given sole credit for the Anthony Campagna estate at Riverdale, New York; the Clarence Dillon estate, Far Hills, New Jersey; the Benjamin Moore estate,

Syosset, New York; the Myron C. Taylor estate at Lattingtown, New York; the grounds of the National Gallery of Art at Washington, D.C.; and the plans for the Queens, New York, community of Fresh Meadows, with architect Clarence Stein.

WARREN & WETMORE

Architects Whitney Warren (1864–1943) and Charles Wetmore (1866–1941) are famous for their masterful design of New York's Grand Central Terminal, as well as a host of elegant hotels, luxury apartment houses, and stately town houses. While not generally associated with either private or public landscape architecture, their relatively small number of country house projects nevertheless include a handsome terrace garden for Moses Taylor at Mount Kisco, New York, and the landscaping and garden design for Crow's Nest, the William K. Vanderbilt Jr. estate at Northport, Long Island. During the firm's first decade, country house design played a more significant role in their work.

STANFORD WHITE
See McKim, Mead & White

Selected Bibliography

Writings by Architects and Landscape Architects

Blossom, Harold Hill. *The Landscape Beautiful.* Boston: Brown, Derby, 1923.

Bush-Brown, James, and Louise Bush-Brown. *America's Garden.* New York: C. Scribner's Sons, 1939.

———. *Portraits of Philadelphia Gardens.* Philadelphia: Dorrance, 1929.

Coffin, Marian Cruger. *Trees and Shrubs for Landscape Effects.* New York: Scribners, 1940.

Dean, Ruth Bramley. *The Livable House: Its Garden.* Vol. 2 of The Livable House, ed. Aymar Embury II. New York: Moffat, Yard, 1917.

Downing, Andrew Jackson. *A Treatise on the Theory and Practice of Landscape Gardening as Adapted to North America.* New York: A. O. Moore, 1841.

Eliot, Charles William. *Charles Eliot: Landscape Architect.* Boston: Houghton Mifflin. 1902.

Elwood, Philip Homer, Jr. *American Landscape Architecture.* New York: Architectural Book Publishing, 1924.

Gréber, Jacques. *L'Architecture aux Etats-Unis.* Two volumes. Paris: Payot, 1920.

Innocenti & Webel. *Selected Projects by Innocenti & Webel.* Greenvale, New York: Innocenti & Webel, n.d.

Jensen, Jens. *The Clearing: A Way of Life.* Chicago: R. F. Seymour, c. 1949.

———. *Siftings.* Chicago: R. F. Seymour, c. 1939.

Lowell, Guy, ed. *American Gardens.* Boston: Bates and Guild, 1902.

Nichols, Rose Standish. *English Pleasure Gardens.* New York: Macmillan, 1902.

———. *Italian Pleasure Gardens.* New York: Dodd, Mead, 1931.

———. *Spanish and Portuguese Gardens.* Boston: Houghton Mifflin, 1924.

Parsons, Samuel, Jr. *The Art of Landscape Architecture.* New York: Knickerbocker Press/G. P. Putnam's Sons, 1915.

Platt, Charles Adams, *Italian Gardens.* New York: Harper & Brothers, 1894.

Root, Ralph Rodney. *Design in Landscape Gardening.* New York: Century, 1914.

Steele, Fletcher. *Design in the Little Garden.* The Little Garden, ed. Mrs. Francis King. Boston: Atlantic Monthly Press, 1924.

Wharton, Edith. *Italian Villas and Their Gardens.* New York: Century Company, 1904.

Monographs

Beveridge, Charles E., and Paul Rocheleau. *Frederick Law Olmsted: Designing the American Landscape.* New York: Rizzoli, 1995.

Brown, Jane. Beatrix: *The Gardening Life of Beatrix Jones Farrand, 1872–1959.* New York: Viking, 1995.

Cortissoz, Royal. *The Architecture of Charles Adams Platt.* New York: Acanthus Press, 1998.

Cortissoz, Royal. *Domestic Architecture of H. T. Lindeberg.* Foreword by Robert A.M. Stern. New York: Acanthus Press, 1996.

Garrison, James B. *Mastering Tradition: The Residential Architecture of John Russell Pope.* New York: Acanthus Press, 2004.

Grese, Robert E. *Jens Jensen: Maker of Natural Parks and Gardens.* Baltimore: Johns Hopkins University Press, 1992.

Hewitt, Mark Alan, Kate Lemos, William Morrison, and Charles D. Warren. *The Architecture of Carrère & Hastings.* New York: Acanthus Press, 2006.

Hilderbrand, Gary R. *Making a Landscape of Continuity: The Practice of*

Innocenti & Webel. Cambridge, Massachusetts: Harvard Graduate School of Design and Princeton Architectural Press, 1997.

Karson, Robin. *Fletcher Steele, Landscape Architect: An Account of the Gardenmaker's Life, 1885–1971.* Sagaponack, New York: Sagapress, 1989.

Kathrens, Michael. *American Splendor: The Residential Architecture of Horace Trumbauer.* New York: Acanthus Press, 2002.

Longest, George C. *Genius in the Garden: Charles F. Gillette and Landscape Architecture in Virginia.* Richmond: Virginia State Library and Archives, 1992.

Metcalf, Pauline C. *Ogden Codman and the Decoration of Houses.* Boston: Boston Athenaeum/David R. Godine, 1988.

A Monograph of the Work of Mellor, Meigs and Howe. New York: Architectural Book Publishing, 1923.

Morgan, Keith. *Charles Adams Platt: The Artist as Architect.* New York: Architectural History Foundation and MIT Press, 1985.

Pennoyer, Peter, and Anne Walker. *The Architecture of Warren & Wetmore.* New York: W. W. Norton, 2006.

———. *Delano & Aldrich.* New York: W. W. Norton, 2003.

Schnadelbach, R. Terry. *Ferruccio Vitale: Landscape Architect of the Country House Era.* New York: Princeton Architectural Press, 2001.

Tankard. Judith B. *The Gardens of Ellen Biddle Shipman.* Sagaponack, New York: Sagapress, 1996.

White, Samuel G. *The Houses of McKim, Mead & White.* New York: Rizzoli, 1998.

General References

American Society of Landscape Architects: Illustration of Work of Members. New York: The House of J. H. Twiss, 1931.

Baker, John Cordis. *American Country Homes and Their Gardens.* Philadelphia: John C. Winston, 1906.

Birnbaum, Charles A., and Robin Karson, eds. *Pioneers of American Landscape Design.* New York: McGraw-Hill, 2000.

Cohen, Stuart and Susan Benjamin, *North Shore Chicago, Houses of the Lakefront Suburbs, 1890–1940,* New York: Acanthus Press: 2004.

Ferree, Barr. *American Estates and Gardens.* New York: Munn, 1904.

Fox, Pamela, *North Shore Boston: Houses of Essex County, 1865–1930,* New York: Acanthus Press, 2005.

Griswold, Mac, and Eleanor Weller. *The Golden Age of American Gardens: Proud Owners, Private Estates, 1890–1940.* New York: Harry N. Abrams, 1991.

Handlin, David P. *The American Home: Architecture and Society, 1815–1915.* Boston: Little, Brown, 1979.

Howe, Samuel. *American Country Houses of Today.* New York: Architectural Book Publishing, 1915.

Jackson, Richard S., Jr. and Cornelia Brooke Gilder, *Houses of the Berkshires, 1870–1930,* Acanthus Press, 2006.

McGuire, Diane Kostial. *Gardens of America: Three Centuries of Design.* Charlottesville, Virginia: Thomasson-Grant, 1989.

Miller, Wilhelm. *The Prairie Spirit in Landscape Gardening.* Urbana: University of Illinois Agricultural Experiment Station Circular, no. 184, 1915.

Morrison, William, *The Main Line Country Houses, 1870–1930,* New York: Acanthus Press, 2002.

Patterson, Augusta. *American Homes of To-day: Their Architectural Style, Their Environment, Their Characteristics.* New York: Macmillan, 1924.

Philadelphia Architects & Buildings, Athenaeum of Philadelphia, www.philadelphiabuildings.org

Pregill, Philip, and Nancy Volkman. *Landscapes in History: Design and Planning in the Western Tradition.* New York: Van Nostrand Reinhold, 1993.

Shelton, Louise. *Beautiful Gardens in America.* New York: Scribners, 1915, rev. ed. 1924.

Index

ACANTHUS PRESS
FINE BOOKS

20TH CENTURY
DECORATORS SERIES

THE ARCHITECTURE
OF LEISURE SERIES

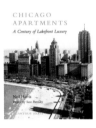 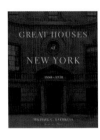 

URBAN DOMESTIC
ARCHITECTURE SERIES

  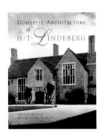

THE AMERICAN
ARCHITECT SERIES

 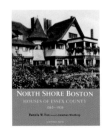 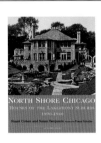

SUBURBAN DOMESTIC
ARCHITECTURE SERIES